CALL ME CHEF, DAMMIT!

CHEF ANDRE RUSH

with Travis Thrasher

CALL ME CHEF, DAMMIT!

A Veteran's Journey from the Rural South to the White House

HARPER HORIZON

Published by Harper Horizon, an imprint of HarperCollins Focus LLC.

Author is represented by the literary agency of The Fedd Agency, Inc.,
P. O. Box 341973, Austin, Texas 78734

Book design by Aubrey Khan, Neuwirth & Associates.

ISBN 978-0-7852-4946-7 (eBook)
ISBN 978-0-7852-4945-0 (HC)

Library of Congress Control Number: 2021951483

Printed in the United States of America
22 23 24 25 26 LSC 10 9 8 7 6 5 4 3 2 1

To my dear mother

*Tears flood my face as I write this. I remember my anger
at you for not letting me know you were dying. You simply
said, "Keep going—you're doing the Lord's work,"
and you kept telling me that until it was too late.*

*You knew if I had stopped,
I would have never become Chef Rush.*

You were all of me.

Thank you, Madear.

CONTENTS

★ ★ ★

PROLOGUE

★　★　★

N ever judge a book by its cover. Everyone has a story, but
you need to take the time to open the pages before truly
understanding someone's life.

So what do you see when you look at me?

My eyes hide a story I thought I would never tell . . . until now.

The smirk on my face is for negativity. I smile then I react. I
combat it with positivity. Always.

I'm a role model. I accept that. If not to anyone else, then to
every kid who looks up to me.

These fatigues were cut and shaped specifically for me. They
were molded and crafted inch by inch and stitch by stitch to
represent a chef jacket. A jacket reminding me of how I became
a chef after I was told repeatedly—denied repeatedly—betrayed
repeatedly—that I could never be one. After I was told I would
never be anything. A cook could only be as good as a cook, and
a cook in the Army in those days meant nothing. I had these
fatigues tailored to a chef jacket to remind me of the humility
in a job I thought I would never do and the respect in a title I
never thought I would carry.

The medals on this chef jacket remind me of the country that
I served and that I continue to serve. I pinned on these medals
and badges to remind me what I've been through and why.

They aren't for others to see or hear about. They are reminders of my pain and my purpose.

The American flag reminds me every day, "This I defend." Not just this country, but every country. You are all my brothers and sisters.

The USACAT badge represents the U.S. Army Culinary Arts Team and the blood, sweat, and tears it took to be asked to join it. I pay homage to this small team, because it says a lot about the person who earns a place among these chefs. I wasn't a culinarian, and I wasn't the best chef, but I was the hardest worker.

The Bronze Star records triumph and tragedy. I remember vividly why I earned it, and it's a reason that I don't ever share.

The Legion of Merit recalls a medal given to an NCO that they didn't want to give it to. I was that NCO.

It's not about the medals or badges, but about the respect of me accomplishing something. About the service that I gave. The military is like life, with egos and alpha males and pride and power. Some people don't think that you should have the same respect or dignity that they have. They need to believe that they're above you, whether it be through medals or rank or whatever other bullshit they might deem important.

These arms that I've spent a lifetime carving out—these twenty-four-inch biceps caged inside these customized fatigues—are crossed to block out any negativity. My arms are twenty-four inches because they grew from coping, lifting seven hundred pounds out of anger, performing 2,222 push-ups every day to help those who gave up, who think about giving up, and who need help. Those push-ups are to help myself too.

My clenched hands and stern smirk are meant to keep the doubters and haters at bay.

My hands are held, to remind me to control myself. I hold them tight every day. My knuckles are bruised permanently to remind me where I came from.

I wear this chef coat with pride, just to let everyone know, "*I'm a chef, dammit!*" It represents my struggle to do something that a kid from Mississippi was told he could not do. It sends a message that you can do what you want to do and be just as influential doing it.

My PTSD I talk about is a gift and a curse. I've mastered making thousands of dishes over the years, but I've learned there is no recipe for coping with trauma. Like life, it's your choice on how to deal with it. Anybody who suffers from PTSD has their own battle to fight. Yet sometimes it's hard to take up arms since we can't even see the war raging inside of us.

With help and with time, you can control it. But you can't do it alone.

So that's all of the outward stuff you see, the stuff that's on the cover of the book; these are the things I share on social media. Now I'm finally going to open up and allow you to hear about my personal stories, the tales that made me Chef Rush. The saga about a sickly kid being forged in the Army and finding a passion in the culinary arts. A journey through military bases, the Pentagon, and the White House to the aftermath of surviving 9/11. A life led under the radar until a simple picture posted on social media changed that life forever.

This is what you can't see. Cooking was a hobby for me until it later saved my life, giving me hope I could share with others. I would take a bullet or give a bullet for any of my principles. I would do a mission, then come back and cook a five-star meal. I loved to fight, not for the violence but for the release. It was an outlet, and still is. So when people ask why a chef needs to be that big, I give a simple reply: *To whup yo ass!* Then feed you dessert.

This book isn't an autobiography that's going to bore you with a diary of specific dates and details related to my life as a chef and military veteran. My point in sharing my life story with you is to let you know that you can do anything you want to do. When I show up, I tell people, I'm here and I'm going to make you uncomfortable. I'm going to give you everything I have. Everything I know. All my mistakes and mishaps and misdirections. Everything. I've wanted to be an open book because so many have kept theirs closed to me.

So keep reading, dammit!

A BOY CALLED HORSE

You are the sum total of everything you've ever seen,
heard, eaten, smelled, been told, forgot—it's all there.
Everything influences each of us, and because of that
I try to make sure that my experiences are positive.

MAYA ANGELOU

The pounding woke me up in the early morning. It was a violent *bam bam bam* on the door, echoing like machine gun shots. They weren't coming just from the front of our home but from multiple doors in our community. Our family had moved from the south-side projects of Columbus, Mississippi, to these north-side projects a few years after I was born. It was like going from nothing to nothing. The north-side projects did have a more tightly knit, family atmosphere, with two units residing in one building and multiple buildings spaced closely together. The loud knocks woke up everybody.

My four older sisters jumped out of bed, and I quickly followed. They were all teenagers, the youngest ten years older than me. There were eight of us children. I had an older brother who passed away before I ever met him, and my only other brother was twenty years older than me. The baby of the family, Tomasina, was a year younger than me.

As we all gathered around the door, I could see Mama looking startled. We wondered if somebody was about to burst through the door.

"Stay back," she told us.

After pausing for a few moments, my mother opened the door. Nobody was there to be found, but there was a note left on the floor. My mother picked the note up and began reading it aloud. I can still hear her reading it.

Dear Niggers: Thank you for doing our jobs for us. Thank you for killing yourselves, and thank you for being so ignorant. You know, we expect nothing from you niggers—

My mother stopped reading. It had two or three paragraphs, but she was finished sharing it with us. The damage had been done, however, because my older siblings were furious. Especially when we realized that other people in our community had gotten the same sort of letters. Handwritten messages of hate.

As everybody filed out onto the lawn between the buildings, I felt the morning dew on my bare feet. There was a hint of daylight breaking on the horizon. It was just dark enough that somebody pulling this sort of hateful act could run away without being seen or caught. Grandmothers and mothers stood in their nightgowns talking while kids still were groggy from just waking up. As a young kid, I didn't understand why everybody was so angry. I didn't know what the commotion was about, and why people wanted to find whoever wrote it.

This was the day I learned "nigger" was a hate word.

Hearing a letter like that had an effect that it might not have today. The word meant something different back then. It carried the weight of the world on its shoulders. In Mississippi back then, there was literally just black and white. Racism was real and it was raw. "Nigger" was not just a word; it was a weapon. Now when you hear this word, it can sometimes be used as a term of endearment that blacks use toward one another. It's used so often it's become diluted. There are those who feel entitled to say it but know others can't dare utter it. Back then, "nigger" held so much weight that it would keep you from breathing. I don't use that word as either an endearment or an entitlement.

When we were back inside, my brothers wanted retribution and talked about what they would do if they found the culprits. My mother wasn't having any of that.

"You're not doing anything," she said. "You're going to sit here. You're going to do what you always do and live for another day."

My mother was a very kind woman, and she wasn't someone to feed off of a situation like this. Among many other things, Emma D. Rush was a midwife at one time in her life. I love my mother to death, but I grew up to be angry at her sometimes; I'm angry because she was the one who put so much fucking love in my heart, so much that it made it hard for me even to this day to look at people with hatred.

This was the 1970s, which was a difficult period for racism. The Ku Klux Klan was still active, and we eventually discovered they were behind the notes. The kids talked about doing something, but nobody could do anything. We were young and I was just starting to understand the reality of racism, the ignorance behind racism, the damage it does, and the heartbreak I felt when I knew I couldn't insulate my family from it. At the time, I was a follower, looking up to my brothers and sisters, so I thought, *If they're angry, I should be angry.* But my mother was telling me I shouldn't be angry, and she explained why.

Hatred and anger came from emotions.

"Emotions can save lives and emotions can take lives," Mom told me. "Emotions can put you in jail and emotions can make you do things that you can't take back."

My mother tried to explain that being emotionally destructive is feeding off something that somebody wants to happen. She knew that these letters were meant to cause a reaction, but that reaction, back then, would have been suicide.

"You can't just react to things you don't know anything about," my mother told my brothers and sisters.

We didn't have weapons and we didn't have people to join us in combat. We were just a bunch of families in the projects trying to make a living. And trying to stay alive.

★   ★   ★

While my mother showed me how to love, it was my father who showed me how to work. Harder than everyone else.

"Dre, let's go," he would tell me before leaving to go work on a farm.

Tommy Lee Miller was a very aggressive man, very dark-skinned. I remember veins in his arms that were as big as your fingers. He called me "Dre," not in an affectionate tone but rather in a stern and direct manner. As a kid it sounded harsh—even scary—whenever my father said it. He worked in construction for fifty years, and this was when construction was real construction, with fewer machines and more manual labor getting the job done. My father's brawny physique proved this. Even though he could be the nicest man in the world, his persona felt so dominant to me, so intimidating. While he also worked as a truck driver, his most important job was to teach me my work habits and work ethic. Little did I know he was showing me how to be a man.

As was true among most of the families I knew in the projects, my dad and my mom weren't married. I didn't know what marriage was. Maybe one or two families had couples who were legally bound, but all I knew was *that's your mom and your dad.* That's how it was. My dad was always there.

As soon as I could walk, my dad put me to work. He came to the house every day or every other day and I would climb into his dirty and rusted-out truck that he drove to one of the local farms. One day I asked him why we needed to go to work.

"When I was eight years old like you, I had to drop out of school to help my mom and dad," my dad said. "That's how I got these rough hands. That's how I learned how to build the first house I ever finished."

I had seen a picture of my grandfather, taken on a farm. It was a grainy black-and-white photograph, and the image reminded me of one of those stereotypical movies depicting a very dark-skinned man working on some sort of plantation. My grandfather was lean but muscular, and I could see my father's reflection when I looked at the photo.

After working at his regular job, my father took me and my siblings to different farms to help him in the fields, picking peas, tomatoes, corn, and green beans, and heaping them in thirty-pound, brimming bushels. I even had the pleasure of picking cotton. It hurt. It hurt a lot. But I always did everything my dad asked me to do. My dad was so in tune with the earth, and he tried to teach us how to be this way.

"Dre! Pick it like this. You gotta do it this way, Dre."

I would be holding a dirty vegetable in my hand and my father would say, "Taste it, Dre! What does it taste like? Just bite it!"

Like a gourmet chef sampling a succulent dish behind a giant stove, I sampled the ingredient. I didn't want to bite a dirty vegetable, but I did. I didn't like vegetables, but I would learn much later that we didn't eat a lot, so these vegetables were pretty damn good. Soon I would be eating vegetables before going anywhere, and I would eat so much that my father finally had to start saying, "Dre, stop eating all the food!"

Some days, as I walked beside Dad under the searing Mississippi sun, seeing the beads of sweat on his forehead, I listened to him mumbling things, whether to himself or only for me to hear. We didn't have a radio or anything else to listen to, but that was okay because I enjoyed hearing him talk. He spoke to me with the passion of a preacher, and I soaked in the words as if I were listening to Martin Luther King Jr. give one of his most memorable speeches.

"Do you see this soil?" he asked as he began to dig in the dirt, pulling out a long and twisting worm. "Did you know that even earthworms provide all the nourishment we need?"

"You don't eat worms," I said.

"Sure you do. They're high in protein and lots of other things." Then he took that dirty worm and ate it like it was nothing.

The first time he ate a worm, I couldn't believe it. Sometimes I think he ate the worms to show me they were God's gift to us. It was pretty funny and disgusting at the same time. Little could I have imagined that years later, I'd be doing the same thing with real bugs while I was in the military.

The gravitas my dad carried with his dogged work ethic came from the fact that he was old to have a young kid. All of my brothers and sisters were much older than my younger sister and me; by this time in his life, my dad could basically have been our grandfather, and he spoke as such. His words resonated with the wealth of a lifetime of memory. He had already gone through two decades of seeing his children grow, so he could reflect on this and teach me. I know now this was why he was so hard on me, and why he made such an impact on me. He pushed me in ways he never pushed his other kids.

The bushels we filled weren't only for our family but for others. Sometimes we helped strangers pick bushels, and at the end of our work I watched them drive off with them in the back of their trucks. At the time I didn't understand why we went to different farms and picked all these things. When we had visited white farms, I had seen machinery for picking vegetables, so why then were we picking all these by hand, bit by bit and piece by piece? One day my dad explained.

"Dre. Do you know why we're doing this?"

"No, sir," I replied. "I know that we're getting some food. I know we get some vegetables."

He shook his head, his eyes piercing me. "This is what we're supposed to do. We help each other, grow from each other. We learn from each other. We pick for each other. This is a community. This is what we do."

His dark ebony hand pointed at the farm we were walking across.

"You see me doing it for the black man. You see me doing it for a white man. You see me do it for my family. You see me doing it for us."

This was Mississippi, and back then the world was painted in a very distinct black and white way. There was no in between, so sometimes when you were spoken to as such, you could tell by the way people talked to you. When I heard a white person talking to my dad, the tone sometimes sounded degrading and dismissive. My dad always answered with a "Yes, sir" spoken as a sign of respect but not one of submission.

I grew to understand that we were part of a community, and my dad wanted me to learn that we all needed to keep going and keep strong and never forget where we came from. Going to these fields to pick vegetables was more than a simple part-time job; it helped me understand a greater purpose in life. The food this work produced ended up representing something far bigger than a meal.

The older I became, the more I realized that these weren't just my meals for the day. I was sharing a little food with nine or ten people. Sometimes my mother would also share a portion of our meals with homeless people who came through. She never hesitated to invite them into our house to come and eat. I would see a stranger suddenly at the dinner table, and they would be so dirty. Nobody but my mother ever gave them anything.

I recall one man who my mother invited in. He was so filthy and he smelled like a latrine. My sister and I were the only ones living with my mom now, and I remember us hiding behind a couch and peering over to look at him. We were wondering why she let him into our home. My mother gave him a little bag of stuff and then he left. I was still scared when the stranger left, but my mother came up and explained why she had let him come inside.

"You know, Andre, everybody needs help. Everybody is human. You need to take care of everyone. Some people need a little more help than others."

My mom said a lot of things like that. As I've shown, she was an incredible woman. My dad's philosophy was different. He would look at a stranger and say, "Hey, you gonna work for it. You got legs you walk on all day, so you can put them to good use."

Love others and work hard. Those phrases sum up my mother and father, and they pretty much sum me up too.

★ ★ ★

"Can Andre come out and play?"

I heard my friends at the door of our home talking to my mom. Her response was one she had given them many times before.

"I'm sorry, but he's not feeling well enough today."

Soon I heard voices by my bedroom window. It was the middle of the summer, and the July sun lit up the day, but there I was stuck in bed, sweat covering me and a nose leaking mucus. I heard voices calling my name.

"Andre, you okay?"

My friends could see me through the glass. All I did was shake my head. My voice was too weak to even reply. This wasn't the first time I'd gotten the flu, but on this particular occasion, I felt like I was going to die.

Why am I always gettin' sick? I wondered.

I was an extremely quiet kid when I started attending school in first grade at Union Academy. I never said anything and never caused any commotion or got into trouble. It was a very small school full mostly of black kids from the projects along with a few from surrounding neighborhoods. Along with being quiet, I was a sickly kid. For some reason I would get sick, and no one knew why. I would wake up with a fever or feel run-down, but the doctor always said he couldn't find anything. I knew there was more, but nobody ever tested me. All I wanted was to know what was wrong, to have an answer, but I never got one.

My younger sister always commented on my health. "You always sick, boy. Everything you do—sick, sick, sick!" That winter while I was in first grade, it snowed for the first time in Mississippi. My mother told me and my younger sister to stay inside, but I wanted to go outside so bad just to experience actual snowflakes for the first time. My older brother and sister were playing in the winter wonderland, so they snuck us out of the house. I snuck out without a coat or a hat, and since I was such a sickly kid, guess what? A snowflake flew in my ear and I got an ear infection. It was my first ear infection, and since I was a young kid, that made it a billion times worse. I was out of school for an entire week, all while having to hear my mother say, "Didn't I tell you to stay inside?"

First grade was full of bad kids. I wasn't one of them. We had a lot of class clowns and disrespectful students, ones who were always getting in trouble for talking in class. As the boy who never said much and wanted to connect with my fellow classmates, one day I decided to try to connect by being funny. When our teacher asked me, "What is your town?" I told her, "Fred's." Since we lived in the projects, Fred's was the place we went to when we said we were going to "town." The teacher thought my joke was serious.

"What do you mean Fred's?" she asked. "You don't even know the town you live in?"

Several of the kids laughed while she realized I was trying to be silly, so my teacher took me down to the principal's office.

That year, I failed first grade. I remember my teacher talking to my mom for some reason, and I didn't know why since I didn't have bad grades. She had told my mother that I had a learning disability and I needed to be held back before I went to second grade. My mom believed her, so she came to me and shared it in her gentle, sensible way.

"Andre, your teacher told me you're so smart that they want to keep you in first grade again next year."

I simply went along with it, saying, "Okay, Mom." I didn't know what first grade was supposed to be like.

When I ended up going to second grade, the same thing happened again: the teacher told my mother there was something wrong with me, that I had learning deficiencies. My mother agreed to have me held back *again*, so I ended up repeating second grade.

I just knew something wasn't right.

My younger sister was very smart, and basically everybody around me was intelligent, but I knew I wasn't *not* smart. I couldn't blame my mom for buying into their decision. She had all these kids to worry about, so she had her hands full. Mom even came and asked me if I was having problems at school, if anything was wrong, but I simply told her, "No, ma'am."

By the time third grade rolled around and they tried to pull the same stunt again, using words with my mother like "dyslexia" and suggesting I be put into special ed, I had no idea what was the matter. It didn't make any sense. All I could think was *I don't know what you're talking about! I'm just a kid.*

I had never heard my mom curse in my life, but when she was told I would have to repeat third grade, she made an exception.

"They're fucking lying," Mom yelled. "This is not fucking right."

By this time, my sister who was a year younger than me had already passed me by. Mom held her ground and refused to let me repeat another grade. She went to the principal and yelled and screamed at him. She ended up discovering that the school had treated a couple of other black kids like this. Kids from the projects, ones who could easily be overlooked and dismissed. Kids with no learning disabilities whatsoever.

It was later learned that this was purposely done to kids by teachers, especially the kids who were disorderly. But I never wanted to be noticed—I was a quiet kid. Maybe they did this to me to impact statistics and fill the spaces to get more funding.

Sometimes I wonder what would have happened if I didn't repeat first and second grades. Those decisions changed the entire course of my life. Would I be here right now writing this book? Would I be known as Chef Rush, helping lots of people, or would I be a chef at all? Would I have any platform at all?

The truth is I don't think about things like that. In fact, my younger sister had to jog my memories of what happened to me in grade school. I had blocked those memories. I have a tendency sometimes to do that to things that have affected me in a dramatic way. Trust me, there have been a lot of those things in my life. I know who I am and I live in the here and now. Some people like to dwell in the past, wondering what might have been if they had made this decision or if something had worked out for them. Some people carry regrets around with them like holding on to a genie in a bottle after making three wishes. I don't wish to change anything in my past, simply because that's impossible to do.

All I know is that you can change something in your life today.

Reflecting on being held back in those grades, I realize a powerful truth. No one decides your destiny. Your destiny decides you. And it's up to you to mold it for your needs and others'.

★   ★   ★

My mother was the best cook in the world. She planted the seeds inside of me that would grow into my becoming a chef, not just with the dishes she made but with the way she delivered them to our family. Southern food always came hand in hand with southern hospitality. My mother was the epitome of hospitality, showing it with neighbors and friends; she served us comfort food, which came with a lot of calories and a whole lot of care.

When my family came together around the table, I got to spend time with my brothers and sisters. Sharing meals felt like a whole different world. We ate and laughed and talked. The food was amazing and so was the camaraderie. Every time we came together, we prayed, we stayed, we loved, and we were grateful. Afterward, we would go back to squabbling as usual, never losing sight of how much we loved each other. I always wanted to hold on to those feelings around the table; that's another reason I ended up becoming a chef.

It was ironic that in a family with five girls, it was the two boys who ended up learning and loving to cook. I had to sneak in the kitchen to cook because my father disapproved. "Dre, men don't cook!" he told me. "They don't do that." But I didn't listen to him. Mom would secretly let me cook, and my brother Ricky also taught me a lot in the kitchen. They both inspired my love for the culinary arts. It turned out my father didn't know I became a chef until shortly before he passed away.

I was a mama's boy; I held a fierce love for my mother. I liked being around her, so naturally I wanted to learn from her in the kitchen. Plus I could get another little taste of the food. I loved to see the joy and passion she took from cooking. It was real. Everything she made seemed so marvelous. The smell of the caramel she made from scratch. A chocolate cake that she made without measurements that turned out so moist. The chicken she cooked that had all those tender juices dripping from it. "Why does your food taste like this?" I asked her. It wasn't just the recipes she used or the routine she had. There was something magical about her meals.

One day my mother let me cook a meal for my friends. I was young, but I was by myself. It was a simple meal consisting of a steak and some vegetables. My friends came over and ate it, and one of them told me I could really cook. I know it probably tasted like garbage, but all I was trying to do was replicate what my mother did in the kitchen.

I didn't realize that in the South, you eat differently. I never knew how different dining experiences could be demographically until I joined the military. What makes southern food so amazing is the hospitality. Service makes food taste better. I've tasted many dishes in many places with many prominent people, but if the service is not on par, then nothing else matters. That fine, fattening southern food was delicious, but what made it special was that it was smothered with love.

My mother showed me how to cook. It didn't start with a recipe but with respect to others. She paid attention not only to the ingredients of her dishes but also to the people who were going to enjoy it. Whether she was serving her sons and daughters or a complete stranger, Mom always showed love and affection with the food she made. She instilled in me the same desire with the meals I would go on to create. It didn't matter if they were presidents and kings and queens or homeless people. Hospitality means putting your heart into your work, every single time.

★ ★ ★

Silent and sickly, I attended my first few grades unseen and unheard, and that's exactly how I liked it. The change that would come over me like a tsunami began in grade school, when I lifted something so heavy that it shocked all my classmates. The feat was completely over-the-top, something none of the other kids could do, not even the older ones. One of my best friends said, "Man, you're as strong as a horse. And you run like one too!" He used those exact words, so then someone else chimed in and said, "Oh yeah, you're Horse now." The next day when they saw me, they called me Horse, and it just stuck.

Despite my new nickname and my newly discovered strength, I remained quiet. It's easy to bully the quiet kids.

During my years in elementary school, I always got bullied. For no reason except that I was quiet and kept to myself, and I never fought back. I wasn't big and hadn't gone through my growth spurt, so I was an easy target. In fifth grade, there was one particular kid named Roosevelt who loved to terrorize me. This kid was big, and he always sat behind me in class, kicking my desk all day long. Everybody watched it like it was some sort of sideshow. When he flicked spitballs on the back of my head, I turned around and told him to leave me alone. This would just make all the other kids laugh.

One day when the teacher left the room, Roosevelt went back to his regular antics, throwing another spitball on the back of my head. As usual, I told him to leave me alone, only to feel his boot pound against the back of my wooden school desk. This time I jumped up and looked back at him. "I said leave me alone." Roosevelt stood up, causing the whole class to react. He was known for beating up everybody, so now it was my time to get pounded on.

Roosevelt didn't wait to talk. His arm reached back as he cocked his fist, then he punched me with all his hefty might, landing a perfect hit right in my jaw. My head cocked and my entire body jerked to one side, but then I balanced myself upright and stared right back at him as if he had never hit me in the first place.

He was dumbfounded. But maybe not as dumbfounded as I was.

Seeing my reaction, Roosevelt darted out of class, afraid of being shown up even more. The rest of the class all went "wooooh" and laughed and talked about what had happened. Outside in the hallway, the teacher stopped him and told him to get back in the classroom, but the kid refused. "I'm not going back in there," he told our teacher. She didn't understand, so she told him he might as well go to the principal's office. He chose that instead of coming back in the same room as me. The next day, the teacher moved his chair over to the other side of the class. Surely she had heard about the altercation.

★　★　★

In the projects, we were all family. We would go to bat for each other. We weren't just friends and neighbors; we were a tribe who took care of each other. As with any family, there was a lot of love, but there could be some pain too.

When I was in elementary school, we would walk to school a mile away from home. My best friend and I would walk together and talk while my younger sister, Tomasina, followed behind us. "Stay behind me!" I told her. She was only in first grade. One afternoon, we decided we were going to go over to another friend's house to play a game, so I told Tomasina to walk home by herself, but she refused. She didn't want to be alone.

"Just go straight down this street," I told her. "You'll be fine."

She was terrified and started to cry, but we took off anyway. When Tomasina arrived back home, my friend's grandmother spotted her and asked what was wrong. By the time we got home, his grandmother was waiting for us. My mother wasn't there, so she brought us both into her house and told us we should have never let my sister walk home alone. She had pulled off branches from the trees and braided them, making them stronger and tighter. Then she commenced to beat us one at a time with those switches. With every swing you heard a *whoosh!*

I went first and then my best friend followed. I will always remember watching him get his ass torn into by his grandmother and hearing him cry his ass off. I couldn't believe it because the switch hadn't hurt me a bit. When we finally went back outside, I was laughing at my friend, assuming he was just acting upset to play it off in front of his grandmother.

"What're you laughing at?" he said.

"What do you mean? That didn't hurt?"

We almost got into a fight, because the switch sure hurt my friend, but he had never been whipped by Emma D. Rush. His grandmother later told my mom that she whipped both of us for what we did to Tomasina. This time it hurt!

It was like this every day in the projects. We were all kindred souls and connected. If someone other than your own parent could give you a whipping, you sure better be family.

★   ★   ★

One late afternoon when I was in fourth grade, my father and I walked along a dirt path cut between two fields. The bushels of peas and corn were full and loaded in his truck. Before we reached his truck, my father stopped and pointed at the ground.

"Dre, you see that penny there? Pick it up!"

"Pick it up?" I replied with a chuckle. "It's a penny."

"And I said pick it up."

I picked up the dirty penny and slipped it into my pocket.

"One thing you gotta remember, Dre—money doesn't grow on trees," my dad said. "You can't go pick it up in a farm, Dre. You have to work for it. Every penny you work for."

This was my father's story, the narrative of his life. He worked extremely hard and developed this habit in me. He also showed me what to do with the money he earned. We lived a very simple life. I wore shoes for two or three years. I rarely could get haircuts and didn't ever buy new clothes. This prompted kids at school to laugh and make fun of me.

It wasn't that we didn't have the money, but the little bit we had needed to go to other places and people. Even as a kid I was okay with that. Eventually I grew to respect my father's attitude with financial matters.

The irony of it is to that very day, I still pick up pennies. I haven't stopped. I still put them in a piggy bank. Those piggy banks have turned to stocks, and those stocks turned into money marketing.

★ ★ ★

The lessons we learn during our childhood are like the lines on our palms. They inform our head and our heart, directing what we do for the rest of our lives. The lessons my dad taught me were etched into my hands, but sometimes they cut more deeply. They demonstrate how life can change in a split second.

One day while doing construction, my dad had an accident and needed to see a doctor. I went to bed that night before he got home. The next day, my dad was sitting in a chair and told me to come over beside him.

"Look at this here," my dad told me, holding out one of his dark and rough hands.

When I looked at the hand, I could see that part of his ring finger had been cut off. I gasped and asked what happened.

"This happened at work," he said nonchalantly, holding up his hand. "I was working on one of the machines and turned my head and just like that it got cut off. In a split second, the saw took it. They couldn't save my finger—they couldn't do anything with it 'cause it was too mangled. This is what happens when you're not careful."

His face didn't appear angry or sad. In fact, he actually looked relieved in a way.

"The good thing is that it was cut off right at the nub. So I can still wear my ring."

For years, my father's missing finger felt like some sort of trophy to him. The older I got, the more I understood why. Whenever I touched my dad, his skin felt like a cross between a bull and a pigskin. The texture was hard and coarse and weathered. His hands especially. They felt like they had been forged in fire. And he always wanted me to understand how the most scorching flames produced the strongest force inside of us.

My dad believed a very long time ago that I was a special kid, so he prepared me for the future that awaited. He didn't have to look at my palms to predict my future. He could see the hard road lined up in the distance and the harsh fates awaiting me, so he forged me to be ready.

REVENGE ISN'T ALWAYS SWEET

Greatness lies not in being strong, but in the right using
of strength; and strength is not used rightly when it
serves only to carry a man above his fellows for his own
solitary glory. He is the greatest whose strength carries
up the most hearts by the attraction of his own.

HENRY WARD BEECHER

"Dre, go over and try to pick up that bucket."

As early as I can remember, my father wanted me to demonstrate my strength. When I accompanied him to the farms to work, he tested how much I could lift, and as the years went by, he continued to do this. Sometimes the feat would be impossible for my younger self, but I always took on the challenge. When I couldn't lift something, it frustrated me. *Next time,* I always told myself. *Just ask me again.*

Perhaps my nickname inspired my father to test the limits of my strength. As I became a teenager, my father knew just how strong I was becoming. One day he gave me a ridiculous dare.

"Dre, try to move that car," he told me.

Is he kidding?

"Go on, move it," he told me. "Try to pick it up."

It wasn't the biggest car, but there was no way I could make the car even budge an inch. I struggled and put all my weight into pulling on the back. My father just looked at me without saying anything. That was my relationship with my dad. Few words and lots of expectations. Few smiles but lots of stares. I eventually gave up trying to lift the car. A month later, my father asked me again, and I failed once again. I hated this because I felt like he was growing angrier at me.

Just give me one more chance, I thought to myself. *Let me try one more time.*

Sure enough, one day I did manage to pick the back of the car up off the ground. After so many tries and so much struggle, I finally did it. My father just looked at me without any acknowledgment. There was no "great job" or pat on the back. Instead, he found a way to disparage my victory.

"It took you long enough," my father told me.

The words weighed more than the car I had been able to move. Grown men couldn't have done what I did. Yet all I got was an "It took you long enough."

Like seeds planted by my mother with her warmth and hospitality in the kitchen, other seeds were sown in me by my father, seeds of dogged determination to drown out the voices of dissent. I began to feed off negativity and find a source of strength inside of myself from it. I blocked out the things in my life that I couldn't do anything about, like being held back in school, while I battled the things I could. My father forced me to grow up and rely on myself, and that's exactly what I did.

★ ★ ★

"That's the one I was telling you about. That's Horse."

I looked across the park to see Roosevelt talking to the group of older boys he hung around with. My former fifth grade bully was smart, because instead of continuing to bug the shit out of me, he decided to befriend me. He knew I was a very strong kid and realized his days of bullying me were over. He lived a couple hundred yards down from us, and one day he brought around some older kids, some who had dropped out of school. Rough characters who did a lot of bad stuff. Really bad stuff.

"Hey, Horse," Roosevelt called out. "Let them see how strong you are. They want to wrestle."

"Man, I'm not gonna wrestle you or anybody else," I told him. But sure enough, after some good-natured taunting and teasing, we ended up wrestling, and every time I beat whoever I was up against. It was never competitive or even close.

This happened at school, too, with fellow sixth and seventh grade classmates challenging me. Whenever we wrestled, I beat them, and they knew I beat them. They were the ones writhing in pain while I was not even using much of my power. It didn't matter that I was still fairly small in size. I pinned down every single guy who wanted to wrestle me. Even the ones who actually wanted to fight.

One day at our school, they brought in a wrestling coach for our PE class, a former wrestler in college who now worked and trained at another school. As he began to talk to us about the sport of wrestling, I had no idea what he was talking about. I didn't even know that this was a legitimate sport. I didn't know about moves like the half nelson, the double leg takedown, or the huddle up. Our school didn't do wrestling. After talking for a few minutes, the coach asked for a volunteer, and everybody called out my name.

"Get Horse!"

So I walked over to him and he gave me a grin.

"I want you to get on your knees and hold your hands," the man told me. "I want you to try not to move. I'm going to do what I can to move you."

I took the position he told me to take and then braced myself as this grown man and professional wrestler attempted to flip me over. We were locked in the over-under position and he was trying his best to gain the advantage and either toss me over or try to pin me down, but it didn't happen. This grown man couldn't move a seventh grader. I was too strong. This continued to happen, with different kids trying to challenge me, but the result was always the same.

I knew I was strong. It would take standing up to another bully to make me realize I was special.

★　★　★

When I was six years old, an older kid named Reggie hung around with the rest of the younger kids in the projects. He was around nineteen or twenty years old. Kids my age would be outside during the day talking and playing in the park shooting hoops when this guy showed up. Some of the kids said Reggie was a predator, but I was too young to understand this word. I just knew he sometimes touched other kids, even some of my friends, and one day he ended up touching me. Now, it wasn't like he attacked me or forced his way on me in a sexual way; there wasn't the opportunity for that in broad daylight. But the young man inappropriately touched me in a way that I would never forget.

Seven years later when I was thirteen, the memory remained inside of me, embedded but not erased. I was with some friends, a few who were older than me, and we were driving around the projects I had been living in when I was a kid. I hadn't been there for a long time. These buildings were literally across the tracks, so we would pass over them and then drive down the street to the cul-de-sac, where you would circle and then head back the same way you came in. Since one of my friends had his driver's license, we were cruising in the car, listening to music with the windows down and checking out our surroundings. As we rounded the dead-end street, I saw a guy who looked familiar sitting on the stoop of one of the buildings.

"Who's that?" I asked my friends.

"That's Reggie," one of the older boys in the car told me.

The hairs on my arms stood up as I grew quiet. I didn't say another word about him. On the way home, I kept thinking about the face I saw.

That's him. That's the same guy who touched me.

It was a Wednesday when I saw Reggie. The following night I found myself walking back to those old projects in my old-ass shoes that I had been using for the last year and a half. The projects were ten miles away and my feet hurt, but I didn't care. I didn't tell anybody where I was going and what I was doing. I wasn't quite sure myself. I felt pulled back to the place I used to live, back to the place where a predator lurked.

What if he's doing the same thing to other kids?

There was no question that Reggie was still touching kids. My fear was that he was doing more.

As I walked up to the building I had seen him in front of, I saw other guys standing around. I didn't know who lived there or whether Reggie had roommates. I didn't know anything, including what the hell I was doing there in the first place. Some sort of force had driven my thirteen-year-old self to this doorstep to knock and then wait.

I'd been waiting a very long time for this.

When Reggie opened the door, I looked at him and felt my heart beating like crazy. Beating so fast it might burst out of my chest and take off running down the road. The tall guy looked at me without any recognition.

"Yo, what's up?" he said in a nonchalant way.

A low simmer inside my soul began rising.

"You know me?" I asked. "You know—from the projects. Lived there when I was just a little kid."

"Oh, yeah, you're Ricky's little brother." His eyes moved over me with casual menace. "You sure grown up, didn't you? So what're you doing around here?"

"I saw you the other day," I said.

He nodded and invited me in. I can't be sure exactly what was going on in his twisted mind. Maybe he thought I had forgotten about what he did to me, or maybe he was thinking I could be another victim. As I stepped into his small house, my pulse continued to race and every sense in my body and mind flashed. His place was dark just like the rest of these projects. They made them this way, with dim thirty-watt bulbs that made you feel like you were living in a shadow.

"You want something to drink?" Reggie asked in his smooth tone. "You want a beer?"

That's how it starts. I told him I was fine.

"So what are you doing?" he asked. "What's going on?"

"Nothing. Just came by to see you."

"Yeah?" Reggie asked with a friendly grin.

"Yeah."

Before he could utter another word or nod his head or flash his smile, I grabbed him. For the first time in my life, I realized just how special I happened to be. I could see that I was different. I hit Reggie so hard, I felt my fist going through his skin. My knuckles knew they were cracking bones. By the time the screams rose out of his mouth, I felt like I was hovering outside of my body watching the whole scene unfold as Reggie tried and failed to fight me off. This didn't just feel surreal. This beating felt supernatural.

I didn't come over here to start whipping his ass. I knew I was angry and ashamed at how he had touched me, but I never knew those emotions could turn into this sort of assault. A part of me knew that older people shouldn't harm young kids like that. That me stood in front of Reggie, grabbing his neck and punching him until he crumpled to the floor.

As I saw the battered figure on the floor, I noticed the blood splattered around him. It suddenly hit me what had happened.

What have I done?

There wasn't even a struggle. I did this, and it was so easy. Too easy. I could do more too. A lot more.

It felt like I woke up from a hazy nightmare. I knew I needed to get out of there, so I bolted toward the door and began running back home. For ten miles, I ran as fast as I could in those raggedy-ass shoes that were barely staying together. My mind replayed what just happened. I saw myself hitting Reggie the way a character might on television. It felt like I had been playing a video game and not really striking down a person.

When I got home, I quietly went into the bathroom and took off all my clothes to wash myself up. My shirt and jeans were streaked with blood, and so were my hands and arms. I could feel my body shaking under the hot water of the shower. I felt scared.

I worried what was going to happen next. But what really terrified me was the realization of what I was fully capable of doing to another human being.

I didn't say a word to my mother or my family that night, and I didn't say anything to anybody the next day. I remained silent as I waited. One day passed, then another, and no one came looking for me. The cops didn't show up, and neither did Reggie. After a few days, I knew there wouldn't be anybody coming to my door. I never saw the pedophile I beat up ever again, nor did I hear what happened to him.

My mother had shown me that there were times when you had to stop and restrain yourself from reacting. When you couldn't let your emotions take over. But I was old enough to realize that sometimes you needed to do something. Maybe this beating stopped him from harming other helpless kids.

I had a lot more growing up to do, but I knew one thing for certain.

I wasn't helpless anymore. And I could fight to protect other kids like me.

★　★　★

As my strength grew, so did my restraint. I had grown up being bullied, and I always remained silent and kept out of trouble. I never fought back until confronting the predator. Later on, as my size began to catch up with my strength during my teen years, and after realizing what I could do to someone else, this restraint probably ended up saving my life.

Maybe in some way I was trying to model one of my heroes. I had grown fascinated with this show on television called *Kung Fu* starring David Carradine. He played a bald-headed monk making his way through the American Wild West. I loved his attitude toward violence and attacks. For some reason, watching *Kung Fu* inspired me to start to hit myself repeatedly, again and again. I wanted to see how much I could take, how much pain I could endure. I even asked one of my close friends to hit me. I'd even strike my face to test my limits. They never were fully tested. Not ever.

I loved sports and they were a natural part of growing up. Basketball was one of my favorites, especially since all the kids in the neighborhood played, but I was always the one who was a little bit more powerful when it came to the sport. Dribbling harder, pushing off with more force, faster than the others. Sometimes they would put me in the middle just to block someone going to the basket.

As I began to play football in high school, everybody already knew how strong I was. They knew how much I could bench-press and how I could lift almost anything. Everybody also knew how fast I could run. I was a natural at football because of my power and my speed. My only downfall was that I had to work, and I gave a lot of myself to the job. That's what my father taught me and that's how I've approached everything in my life: to give it my all, whether it's working out or cooking or helping others. Unfortunately, I didn't have the privileges that a lot of other kids had, but I never used that as an excuse. This was just my reality.

I worked at Kmart, which happened to be five miles from our house. I didn't have a car, so I usually had to walk to work. If my sister couldn't give me a ride back home, I'd have to make that trek too. Sometimes my coworkers offered me rides, but I always told them that I was okay, that I was fine walking. I wasn't okay, however. It was embarrassing to have to walk everywhere, to not have a car myself, and to almost never have anybody to drive me to and from work. After a long shift, I walked back home late at night, exhausted and knowing I had to wake up early in the morning for school. Even worse was the fact that there was no food in the house, since it had already been eaten up. The next day, I showed up at football practice with weary muscles and an empty belly.

I was still stronger and faster than any of my teammates.

Since I wasn't there all the time, my coach felt like he couldn't put me in as many games. It upset me, but at the same time I understood it. That's just human nature. I realized I outperformed any of the other players, but at the same time I only gave 25 percent. Sometimes I felt afraid to give 100 percent or anything more than 25 percent. I could have run faster and I could have worked harder, but all those things would have made me stand out, something I never wanted to do.

One day at football practice, we were lifting weights, and I couldn't help but get noticed. We didn't have a gym; back in those days there weren't gyms in Mississippi. The closest we had to one was the YMCA, but they still didn't have much of anything. Our school had a little upstairs room with a bench-press and an old piece of equipment used for doing squats. I didn't know how to bench properly. I had no technique, since there was nobody around to teach me one. But I could bench-press 315 pounds easily. Everybody watched with wonder. They couldn't believe I could lift that much weight, but I knew. By then, my body was talking to me, and I realized what I was capable of.

One thing I noticed at an early age was how my body changed every time I did something. I noticed what workouts could do, what lifting resulted in, what consistent exercise produced. Something I tell people to this day is that if your body doesn't talk to you, then you're not doing it right. My body spoke loud and clear to me even when I was a sickly little kid. I like to think of the analogy of Superman, how he was a sickly child himself with this bad cough, but then, all of a sudden, one day he could go through a building. My body began to speak to me when I was playing football and running track. Every time I did anything, my body seemed to say, "Let's do more." I knew I could take a lot.

★ ★ ★

A book I borrowed from my older brother ended up changing my life. Okay, the book wasn't actually "borrowed"; I ended up hiding it from him so I could tell him later he had "left it" at home.

My older brother, Tony, was in the Navy, and he had started bodybuilding. On a trip home from serving in the Navy, he brought a copy of *Encyclopedia of Modern Bodybuilding* by Arnold Schwarzenegger. This book later became my bible, and Schwarzenegger became my childhood hero, right along with Kwai Chang Caine, David Carradine's character in *Kung Fu.*

Since I wasn't much of a reader, I simply looked at the pictures with awe and tried to copy what I saw. Eventually I began to read the words associated with the images, and this helped me understand my own body and that mind-to-muscle connection that Schwarzenegger wrote about.

Of course, since there was almost none of the shit that Schwarzenegger used was anywhere around me, I began to make stuff and get creative. I felt like the guy from the 1980s show *Mac-Gyver* who was always building something out of nothing.

I could not have imagined that one day I would be honored and blessed to have him as one of my biggest supporters and to work alongside him as an ambassador to thousands of kids all across the country.

The summer I read Schwarzenegger's book, I decided to see what this body of mine could do. To see what I was capable of, what could come of working out. So I began to work out, and for me, working out first meant running. Yes, I was a runner. And since we didn't have a lot of equipment in Mississippi, I did a lot of dips on chairs, ones where you hold the backs of the chairs and go up and down over and over again. The chair sometimes flipped over and landed on my head, but I didn't mind. I'd go and get milk jugs out of the refrigerator and perform a dozen different biceps exercises with them. This accompanied working with my dad on the farms, carrying heavy things. There was no rhyme or reason to the exercises, and I'm 100 percent sure my form was absolutely terrible, but my body was thriving. It needed those stimuli and needed that growth.

By the time school started back up, I was noticed. I walked into school looking like a new student, packing twenty more pounds of muscle. The football coach was astounded by how much muscle I put on. "Dang! Andre, you've packed on the muscle this summer! That's incredible!" Mind you—I was still a kid and I had no idea how I looked or what I had done. I called it my summer body because I had this perfect physique that ended up lasting me until the next summer, when I got ready to do it all over again. That was my body. Unbeknownst to me, not everybody heard what I heard. I believed others were created the same way, that everyone heard their body speaking to them. I could look in a mirror and hear my body telling me what to do. "Okay, Horse. We need to do X, Y, and Z. We need to focus on this and on that. You need to eat this and do this." This was the sort of conversation I had with my body, and when I followed the instructions, I saw the results.

I wouldn't know until I entered the military that others weren't built this way, that a lot of people didn't have any sort of dialogue with their body. By the time I joined the Army, I came in with a competitive drive and a knowledge of my capabilities. If I wanted to gain thirty pounds, I gained them. If I wanted to shed thirty pounds, I lost them. I knew my strengths and rarely showed them.

Every now and then, however, I was forced to reveal what I could really do. I was made to give over 100 percent. The results could be mind-blowing. And even a little terrifying.

★   ★   ★

Maybe they wanted to test my strength. Maybe they just wanted to mess with my mind. Maybe they wanted to bully the quiet boy who kept to himself. Whatever made the crew of guys decide to jump me, it didn't matter. My days of being bullied were over.

I was walking down the road—I was always walking to get around in those days—when three cars raced up beside me and stopped. I was in a white neighborhood, figuring it would be safer to walk these streets to get home from school. I still had about four or five miles to go. The three cars were packed, including a small hatchback that had three or four guys in the backseat. Some of the guys I knew from my high school. They climbed out of the cars and I noticed the bricks and bats in their hands. They were all older guys, and I could see that they weren't messing around. They were all part of some kind of silly gang that called themselves The Disciples and had decided I was on the wrong side of town.

One person in the group was a dark-skinned, skinny guy I knew. He grinned at me and said, "What's up?" in a way that made it sound like he already knew what was up. All I was doing was trying to figure out how to get out of there as quickly as possible. The skinny guy swung at me as hard as he could, and just like I did with the bully from middle school, I took the blow without flinching. I didn't move, didn't do anything. My first instinct was to grab him, but instead, I chose my *best* instinct.

Run, Horse.

So I bolted. They called me Horse for a reason. I stormed away from the guys, and as they started to try to chase me, I heard their astonishment.

"Fuck, that motherfucker's fast!"

"Come on, catch him!"

After a minute of running away from them, I stopped. This was the way my mind worked back then.

That guy hit me. So why am I the one running away?

All of a sudden, I got angry. Not just angry, but furious. I stopped and turned around and waited for them. I could have outrun them, but I didn't want to run away. As the first guy approached, he ran up to me and tried to grab me from down low, but I kicked him and then pushed him aside. Behind him came the remaining mob of fourteen guys, some holding pipes and bricks. For a few moments, there was a vicious and violent melee, with punches being struck against me while I swung back hard and fast. I started hitting and kept hitting and kept striking and swinging and pounding. The mob of assailants came at me at the same time, and in seconds they all began to go down and clear out. One of my punches landed against a guy's jaw, another striking one in the throat. My elbow rammed one of them in the gut. This went on and on until some of the guys were curled over on the ground and the others were falling back, covered with their own fears.

After getting the pile of guys off me, I stood there waiting for another round. Instead, I saw them begin to start scrambling away like scared rats. Then I heard the most ludicrous statement I'd ever heard:

"And don't come back!" the skinny guy called out to me.

They were the ones fleeing the scene and I was the one still standing ready to fight.

When I got back to the projects, my older cousins were waiting to greet me. They had already heard about what happened, how this gang was bragging that they had beaten up a kid from our projects. They hadn't done shit to me. Not one of those pipes ever struck my skin. Their punches didn't faze me a bit, and the only thing I really felt was one of the bricks hitting me. My cousins assumed I was almost dead, so when they saw me they couldn't believe what I looked like.

"I thought you got jumped," one cousin told me.

I gave him a nod. "I did."

"What do you mean you did? They're bragging about jumping you."

"Yeah, they did," I said.

I told them the whole story, so my cousins became enraged and wanted revenge for what happened. I calmed them down.

"I'm good," I told them.

They didn't believe me, however. None of them could understand how I meant what I said. Later on that evening, my cousin showed back up looking serious.

"Horse. Come around to the back. We got something for you."

My cousin wasn't one to joke around. He was older than me and had already served time in prison. When I followed him behind my building, I saw the dark-skinned guy I knew, the one who'd struck me in the face. Several other guys stood around him, making sure he didn't try to escape.

"This the guy who hit you?" my cousin asked.

"Yeah."

"So what you gonna do to him?"

For a moment I stared down my attacker, seeing the pure panic covering his ugly face. Then I just laughed.

"Nothing," I said. "I'm good."

"What? This mother jumped you!"

I glanced at my cousin. "You see me? I'm good."

I turned around and walked away. I knew they weren't going to let the guy go, but I didn't want to stick around to see what happened.

The gang that attacked me never came around me again. In fact, they ended up inviting me to join them. The same skinny kid who punched me in the face came around and asked me about it.

"Horse, you should join our gang," he said.

"I'm good," I told him.

"You've already been initiated. All these guys fucking jumped your ass and they didn't do shit to you."

He told me how they were a family, how they took care of each other, how I needed to become part of them.

"No, I'm not joining a gang," I told him. "I'm cool. I'll be okay."

I was right. I was okay. The gang never gave me any flak after that.

★ ★ ★

Violence surrounded me as a little kid and as a middle schooler, and it remained at my side during my teenage years. This prepared me for the path I would take in the future, for the bloodshed I would witness as an adult.

When I got to high school, Columbus had started to become overrun with drugs. There were several gangs that controlled their sale and distribution. Nobody knew exactly how the drugs started to flow into Mississippi; somebody once suggested it was some guy from out of town who showed up talking and dressing differently and acting like a big shot. All we knew for sure was that with the gangs and the drugs came more violence.

On the weekends, kids gathered together with their parents' cars outside in a field or a parking lot. The older kids hung out in a little club, but often that became cramped and overheated, so they would flood the parking lot too. I remember one weekend, I was with some of my friends in the lot outside of a Kroger grocery store, just hanging out having fun. A fight erupted somewhere around us, but that was nothing unusual. Some sort of brawl would break out on any given night, but this one ended up taking a terrible turn for the worse.

One minute, you're standing there laughing and joking around with your friends, and then suddenly you're seeing a group of guys getting into a fight. Not fifteen guys taking on one. No, a full-fledged brawl with everybody jumping around and punching and even gunshots. But I just stayed there. I don't know what my problem was. It was almost as if I had some sort of death wish or something, because when the melee broke out, I should have done the logical thing that everybody does and gotten the hell out of there. But I stuck around, minding my own business. At least trying to.

One guy I knew, named Chuck, came over to me and urged me to join in the madness.

"Man, they're fighting," Chuck told me. "We shouldn't be fighting."

I followed him over there and watched as he went into the middle of the crowd to break up the fighting. Chuck made everybody stop, telling them to cool down and trying to get them to their senses. We both knew that all of us weren't different. We were all the same, just a bunch of kids fighting for no reason at all. Chuck tried to reason with everybody.

After the brawl ended, me and my friends were leaning on our car, talking with some of the crazy people involved with the fight. Chuck was hanging out with us, finding the same sort of amusement we had at how insane some of the people had become. One angry-faced guy came around the corner and scanned our group, then looked back at the guys following him.

"Dis him?"

"Yeah, that's him," someone said.

The angry guy walked up to Chuck and pulled out a gun, and without hesitating shot him in the head. I didn't have time to blink. I didn't move; I didn't even flinch.

What the fuck just happened?

With the gunshot echoing in my ears, I looked down at the crumpled body and thought, *It wasn't him. This isn't the guy you're looking for.*

When I looked back up, I was peering down the barrel of the shooter's handgun. My mind was trying to catch up with what was happening, but it was still too slow. In the background, I heard someone saying my name.

"No, man, that's Horse," the voice behind me said. "Horse? He good. He's cool."

Still aiming the gun at my head, the guy started to smile. "You lucky motherfucker."

Everybody around me had taken off, screaming and ducking for cover. When the shooter and the rest of his gang took off, some other guys rushed over to grab Chuck and take him to the hospital. But he was DOA.

This wasn't the first time I got caught up in gunfire, nor was it the first time I witnessed someone getting shot. Maybe I shouldn't have been hanging around with these sorts of guys, but I was still a kid, a quiet kid who kept to himself. Maybe I did have a death wish, but I also knew the difference between right and wrong.

★   ★   ★

Things ended up getting so out of hand with the drugs and the gangs and the fighting that our town decided to get all these badass kids together and have a town hall meeting. They even had media covering it. My cousin who was a preacher became involved and helped out with the meeting. The kids who came, they were mean and dangerous. Some of them were friends of mine, but they were still bad as fuck. I attended the meeting with them, showing up at this large auditorium where all these parents and kids were sitting and watching. One of the gang members came up to the podium and spoke into the microphone, demanding this and that. He was only sixteen. I stood up there behind him in my African dashiki, listening to this teenager spout off like some politician running for president.

My cousin the preacher left midway through this guy's speech. He had heard enough. My sister Hattie, who was a teacher, had taken me, and she stayed behind to watch the entire meeting. After several of these violent kids made their threats and demands to the quiet crowd, I walked up to the microphone.

"Why are you adults listening to these kids and what they're demanding? *You're* the adults!"

Then I walked away and walked out of that meeting.

Maybe it was a stupid thing to do, alienating my friends and talking down to them. But they had nothing intelligent to say. They were just airing out tired complaints. When I came off the stage, my sister looked at me and smiled.

"That was a good job," she said.

When we got home, we found my mother upset about what had happened. My cousin had called her to tell her about the meeting.

"I heard Andre was in there with all those kids," she said with disgust on her face.

"Mama," my sister said, coming to my defense. "Andre got up there and spoke up against what was happening."

"He did? So why didn't your cousin tell me that?"

My sister and I didn't know at the time that our cousin had left before I went up to talk. It didn't matter. My mother wasn't surprised. She knew she had taught me the difference between right and wrong. She could see that I understood what good and bad looked like. My mother also understood that strength didn't have to be exhibited by picking up cars or bench-pressing weights. Our greatest strength came in exercising the best muscle we had: our mind.

PAUSE, BREATHE, SQUEEZE

I've had to learn that not everybody does things
my way. But I do expect the absolute best of
everyone around me, and I'm disappointed when
people don't expect that of themselves.

MICHAEL JOHNSON

You are your biggest asset. It took me years to understand that.

When I was a young, extremely introverted, and quiet kid, I used to collect items around the house and create things out of them. It could be anything: rubber bands, paper clips, headbands, boxes, beads. We didn't have much in our family, including toys and games, but imagination overcomes inadequacy. I would use anything I could find, and I discovered that I was good at constructing wonderful pieces that I now realize are art.

I remember having my first art class. I didn't know anything about art or drawing. I discovered I loved to draw, which first began as nothing more than doodling. Soon I began to draw everything around me and all the things I envisioned in my head. There were flying horses and unicorns and dragons and all sorts of other animals. They came alive when I put them down on the paper. I saw them moving and soaring above me. They were creations I could see and talk to.

As I entered middle school, I continued to draw, and my art skills continued to progress. Mr. Dawkins was my seventh-grade art teacher, and he saw my potential. He didn't see the simple portrait of the black kid in front of him; Mr. Dawkins saw deeper inside of me. He provided tools for me to use, and he helped me master them. I learned how to do papier-mâché, how to work with charcoal, how to handle clay. My doodles became more distinct, and the instruments I used became more diverse. I sketched in charcoal and painted with acrylic and watercolors. It would be Mr. Dawkins who eventually managed to get me a scholarship to an art college.

One of my first memorable drawings was of a man I saw in an encyclopedia. I had been thumbing through it at our home and saw this interesting person who looked like a good subject to draw. When I showed Mr. Dawkins, he smiled.

"Do you know who this is?" he asked as he glanced down at the drawing.

"No."

"It's Picasso."

I had no clue I had sketched out the famous artist. It became one of my favorite drawings. With each piece I carefully created, I started to find another part of me. On the blank paper I could make things come alive. I could construct them the way I imagined them to be.

After saving up money from working, I bought myself a large sketchbook, and it became the place where my beloved drawings were held. I filled it with pieces of myself, with everything I could possibly think of. The pictures weren't for anybody else.

I drew for me. By the time I reached tenth grade, the sketch-book had around forty pieces of artwork, everything from water-color to charcoal. One day while I was driving a big old beater of a Buick, I put the sketchbook in the trunk of the car, since several of my buddies were riding with me. I left it there until one of my friends at school asked me about it.

"Hey, Horse. Show us your drawings."

At first I resisted, but I eventually popped open the trunk to grab the sketchbook. The moment I touched it, I could tell something was wrong. When I opened the big sketchbook, pages began to fall out of it. The paper was brittle and broke off, crumbling in my fingers. The entire book started coming apart.

Little did I know that when I stuck the sketchbook in the trunk of the Buick, there was an equally old battery hidden back there that was leaking acid. While I was driving, the acid had spilled all over my sketchbook. Discovering the ruined book destroyed me. It hurt so bad. Those drawings meant everything to me. They weren't random and thoughtless images. They rep-resented years of work, and years of memories. These weren't just regular drawings. They were depictions of my life that I would go and hide and create. They were pieces from my imag-ination. They were people I knew and places I wanted to go. They represented parts of life that fascinated me, like Indians with eagles flying around them. I even had my one and only drawing of my mother.

All of those drawings were forever ruined. I'd never imagined that battery acid could do such a thing.

How could I be so stupid to leave my art book back there?

I decided to stop drawing. If I dwelled on the loss of some-thing I treasured so much, I would only remain angry. I would be wading around in the hurt without anything to do with it. So

I stopped. Actually, I didn't exactly stop. I did something that would be continually repeated throughout my life. Especially throughout my creative life.

I pressed pause.

I learned later that this is the way my mind works when I'm doing something or seeing something. I pause it, and then the next day or six years later, I can press that button again and see it just where I left it.

It would take me another ten years before I would draw again.

★　★　★

Not everybody was like Mr. Dawkins, seeing beyond my size and beneath the color of my skin. For some people, that was all they saw.

Even at a young age, I knew the value of hard work. My father taught me this through his life and by taking me out to work with him. He knew the sad truth, that in a small town in Mississippi, there were absolutely no opportunities for anything. Whatever was going to happen to you in life, you had to do it yourself. It didn't matter how big a dreamer you might be. Being in a city like New York or Los Angeles made the chances of achieving your dreams a hundred times more possible, simply because you have a hundred times more opportunities. Back in those days, you grew up expecting to be working on a farm or going to work for the railroad. Those were the size of dreams for people like my father, for people in Mississippi. But you had to work hard to even achieve that.

The general manager of the Kmart store I worked at when I was a teenager was a tall and rail-thin white guy named Cliff. He was too far up to have anything to do with me, yet whenever he saw me or heard that I was there, he would talk to me around his other managers. It didn't take long for me to realize where he was coming from.

"Hey, Andre," Cliff said. "I see you guys on the football team. I guess none of you boys can play quarterback. You always have to be the runners, huh?"

Cliff knew I was a football and a track star, so he was trying to mess with my mind, talking about how black players couldn't play quarterback. He did this several more times, calling me "boy" when telling me to do something. You could hear the disgust in his tone and see it in his expression. "Go get the rest of them carts, boy," he said. "Finish stacking those boxes, boy." The manager seemed to enjoy showing who was boss, all while displaying utter contempt.

The woman who hired me was also black, and she never said a word to him about his behavior. She would shake her head and say, "Oh, don't worry about it." But the daily demeaning began to take its toll. I was tired. Not just physically tired from the long trips I took back and forth to work, but emotionally drained by all the people who tried to intimidate me and make me feel less than I really was.

In the back of the store was a little room where we would go for our breaks. There was a set of lockers we could use for any personal belongings or meals we might bring to the store. One day while I sat in the break room with another employee, Cliff approached us and began talking to the other guy about me. "Look at this *boy*," he said as he began to berate me. I jumped up and approached him, then punched the locker right behind him, putting a six-inch dent in it. He ran out of the room and called security.

My immediate manager came to the back room and wanted to know what happened.

"Andre, what's going on?"

Her eyes looked at me with trepidation, as if I might do something any second.

"I can't take it anymore," I said to her.

My body was weary walking all the time, all these miles every day, and my managers knew this. They also knew I was the hardest worker they had. Cliff deliberately antagonized me, wanting me to react, to say something.

He wants me to hit him, I realized. *Just so he can get rid of me.*

They didn't fire me for punching the locker. They let me stay. I think it was because they knew I was a hard worker, both inside the store and out. Another manager needed some help at his home, so he asked me if I could come over and work on helping to break down his entire pool. So on a hot summer day, I went to this man's house and worked eight hours of hard labor. Hauling big slabs of concrete all day long is tough for a grown man, much less a kid.

At one point, as I picked up a chunk of concrete, I discovered a wasp nest that seemed to explode with a thousand wasps coming at me. I must have been stung in a dozen places all over my body. Thank God I wasn't allergic. My manager wasn't very sympathetic. I was a big kid and he needed me to help finish the job, so I kept working.

At the end of the grueling day, my manager drove me back home since I didn't have a ride. When we reached my house, he stopped and gave me thirty dollars. He said, "I'm giving you what Kmart pays you and not taking taxes from it, so you're actually making more." That equaled less than four dollars an hour. I knew he was lying and trying to justify how he was taking advantage of me. I knew the labor was worth fifteen dollars an hour, but we had never talked about how much he was going to pay me. Even so, he looked a bit ashamed at the pittance he was giving me.

"I'd give you more, but it's going to cost me a lot to haul off all that concrete from the driveway," he said. "But I got you a sandwich for lunch and took you home, so you can include that."

I nodded and told him goodbye, then climbed out of the car and went inside my home. I gave the money to my mother like I often did, then went and took a shower. The water hitting my skin took off the sweat and the dirt and the grime from the day, but it couldn't touch my disappointment deep inside. All I could do was press the pause button again.

Thirty dollars. That's what they think of my hard work. That's how much they think I'm really worth. A few bucks an hour.

I balled up my anger and buried it. This didn't mean it was gone. It was momentarily halted, but it still remained.

Not long after that, I would press the button again, and the rage would continue to play. I found myself frustrated and furious after another work shift dealing with Cliff's belittlements and bigoted attitude. I decided enough was enough, so I started to follow him out to the parking lot to beat the shit out of him. There wasn't any question anymore about whether he was a racist. He was flaunting it in my face every time I saw him.

Before I could reach him, the woman who hired me came up to stop me.

"Don't you do it," she said. "You're going to ruin your life. If you do this, you will get into trouble. He will call the cops."

"You know who he is," I told my manager. "You know how he acts."

I couldn't believe this black woman was trying to protect him. I was too young and naïve to realize she was really protecting me.

"Let it go," she told me.

"Why does he act that way? Seriously, why? I'm the hardest worker here, but I'm the only person he treats like this. Why?"

"Because you're the best person," she said.

"I don't care if I'm the best fucking person," I said. "I just want the respect everybody else is getting."

I knew I deserved more than being berated and called a boy by this unhappy man full of prejudices. And I knew I was worth more than thirty dollars. I decided to take the advice I had been given and not follow Cliff into the parking lot, but that was the last night I ever walked back home from Kmart. I got fired the next day.

The woman who had protected me was the one to tell me I was fired. Years later she told me she had defended me so I could keep my job, but Cliff had asked her if she wanted to follow me. The kind woman apologized to me when she shared this, but I told her she'd done the right thing. She was a single black mother and had no other choice. People like Cliff didn't give her any other options.

★　★　★

One thing I hated more than almost anything else was having to ask someone for something. Especially my father. I have only borrowed money once in my life, when I asked him as a teenager. It was honestly one of the worst things I ever had to do as a kid. I grew up loathing the very idea of having to ask my dad for something. This was because every time school came around and every single time my sister and I needed school supplies, my father made us come to him and ask for them. I hated having to ask for anything, especially from him.

It took me years to understand why my father did this. He wanted me to know how it felt to ask for something when it wasn't necessary. You wait for those moments and choose them carefully. You ask only when you absolutely have to, and in the case of school supplies, I didn't need to ask because they were going to be given to me anyway. But my father used the opportunity to teach me that I needed to be able to do things for myself before others could, should, or would do them for me. I learned this at a very young age.

The only time I have ever borrowed money was when I asked for $400 to buy my first car, money that I promised I would pay back. I purchased a big beast of a car from an eighty-year-old couple. It was that ugly, four-door Buick. Three weeks after I bought it, the engine caught on fire while I was driving it. After Dad heard what happened, he only made matters worse.

"Dre. Did you have insurance on it?"

"No, I didn't have insurance on it."

I didn't plan on it blowing up in three weeks.

"I paid you back," I said. "I'm okay walking right now."

This was one of those hard lessons from my father, the sort that molded me into the man I am today.

★　★　★

Funny enough, I would end up discovering in high school that I had more family members than I knew about. Flesh and blood family.

My dad was my dad, and I never asked him questions or talked much to him. All my siblings were older than Tomasina and me, and the boys had very different statuses in our family than the girls. My sisters all knew everything about everything in our family. Even Tomasina knew things. But I didn't know shit. I had no idea what was going on with our family. I didn't know who, what, where, when, or why.

One day in sixth grade I was at an important track meet, racing against the Caldwell Bobcats, a rival school. Everybody already knew how fast I was, especially since I beat everybody I ran against. There was a kid I noticed on the other team about my age who was built like me. And he was fast—really fast. They called him Lightning. I thought after hearing his nickname, *What kind of name is that?* Sure, they called me Horse, but I got my name for a reason. They didn't give this guy a name like Cheetah or something like that. No, he was just Lightning.

Even though I ran in the mile and the mile relay, my claim to fame was always the one hundred meters. In high school I would break 10 seconds with a 9.99, a time good enough to make it to the Olympic tryouts. As I walked onto the track that day and entered my lane, I was placed right next to Lightning. By then everybody knew both of us and how fast we were, so people started to talk. As we stretched, I didn't know what the commotion was all about. I was a quiet guy, but this kid, he was arrogant and talked a lot, and everyone loved him. The complete opposite of me. He was confident and was showing it as we knelt into our positions on the blocks.

"On your mark . . . Get set . . ."

The crack of the pistol set us off, exploding up and shooting forward. Lightning and I immediately led the pack. The one hundred is a short and intense race, where every millisecond counts. Thirty meters down the track, the guy was still by my side, and he remained there at forty and fifty meters.

Who is this kid keeping up with me?

We blistered down the hot asphalt toward the finish line, and just as we reached it, Lightning stuck his head out, beating me by the tiniest fraction of a second. When I saw the results, I was pissed off. Furious. I wanted to race again. Now that I knew who I was really up against, I wanted a redo. I knew I could beat him. When I looked over and saw Lightning, it was like the classic high school movie where the stud athlete was celebrating the win with his team. He was surrounded by all the girls. I didn't have girls. I was a poor black kid wearing the same shoes I had to go to work in.

I pressed the pause button and let Lightning go. I forgot about him.

A year or so later, I was hanging out at my friend's house, sitting on his porch where I'd been a few times hanging out with a group. The door opened and a dark-skinned man stepped out, staring at me for a moment as if he knew me. Then he walked past me and got into his car to leave. As his car backed out of the driveway, my friend noticed the interaction.

"Hey, Horse, you know that's your brother," he said.

I looked at him and chuckled. "Fuck you talkin' about?"

"That's your brother Tommy."

I repeated the same line, knowing he was full of it. But as I said, I was oblivious to a lot that had happened in my family.

When I started high school, I was surprised to see the same kid who beat me at that sixth grade track meet sitting in my class. He had a brother and a sister attending our school, and they looked alike—all with the same dark-skinned features. As I was sitting there minding my business, Lightning came up to me and started talking.

"Hey—I remember you," he said. "I'm Tim."

I didn't really want to talk to Tim, but it turned out he was a really nice guy. That was probably one of the reasons he was very popular, and we became good friends. One day in class, Tim was telling me about his family. When he began to talk about his grandfather, I became curious. Certain details sounded familiar. Almost too familiar. There were hints of connections, so I asked him where he was from. When he told me, I knew the truth.

"Can I ask you a question?" I said. "What's your grandfather's name?"

"Tommy Lee," he said.

"That's my dad," I told him.

"Oh shit, you're my uncle."

Tim said this in a surprised but casual way, like it wasn't the craziest thing in the world but rather it was really cool. He immediately embraced me. From that day on, he called me his uncle even though we are the same age. He introduced me to his brother and sister, my newly discovered nephew and niece.

When I got home from school, I immediately told Tomasina the news.

"Hey, I found this out today," I started to explain to her as if I was going to surprise her with my discovery.

"Yeah, I know," she said.

"What do you mean you know?"

"Of course I know about Tim."

She proceeded to tell me all the different connections between my father and his children and grandchildren. I felt so ignorant. I didn't know any of this. And I went almost my entire childhood without knowing part of my family. Sure, my mother and father were never married, but he was still my dad and was treated as such. My foundation was my parents and my siblings; they were the family unit I'd been brought up in. But I accepted the news and enjoyed getting to know these new cousins and nephews and nieces—it was great.

★ ★ ★

One of the family members I deeply loved was my cousin Jayden. Growing up, he was one of the guys I always admired. His mom and dad had a huge house and they spoiled him, giving him anything he wanted. Right after Jayden got his driver's license, his father decided to buy him car. Every time he came and visited, I could tell he was a special kid. A good guy who made you laugh and smile, someone impossible to not like. He would come visit me in the projects, but it was awkward because he dressed and talked differently than my friends, and they let him know it. When his mother passed away when he was sixteen, Jayden snapped. The good kid literally vanished. His mother was the glue of the family, and with her gone, the cousin I dearly loved vanished as well.

His story served as a cautionary tale for me.

After his mother's death, Jayden was allowed to receive the money from her passing. It was her insurance money that went directly to him, based on her wishes. I never understood how his father would allow this. It was around $500 every two weeks. A thousand bucks every single month. I was a kid and I hadn't even seen fifty dollars. So there was Jayden with his car and his monthly grand. All of a sudden, he had all these friends and he began to spend money like it was nothing. He bought all this expensive equipment and music for his car. His dad never stopped him from doing anything, maybe to compensate for his mother not being there.

It was fun to hang out with Jayden. He could come pick me up in his car and we'd drive off somewhere. Remember—I didn't have a car. I was walking everywhere. He was my cousin and I loved spending time with him. He would drink while we were in the car, and sometimes I drank as well. To be honest, I hated drinking alcohol, and sometimes I would play it off, making up an excuse or having as little as possible. My cousin also smoked, something I never did either. I began making bad choices; it's easy to make them when you're with someone you love. Things soon got a bit out of control.

By this time, my mother had moved us out of the projects and into a small house on Martin Luther King Jr. Drive. It wasn't much, but it still was an actual house we were living in. It felt different, as if I had been taken away and now was separated from the rest of my family and friends. Suddenly I was different than everybody else. My cousin would come pick me up and we'd find ways to be reckless. I think about those times now and shake my head. We would be running from cars and alongside trains, so close to experiencing something I call an unnecessary death. That's the sort that is completely avoidable, like when someone riding a motorcycle 150 miles an hour tries to go between two cars an inch apart. So unnecessary.

One day I was in the back of the Morningside projects, hanging out with my cousin on the third floor. They had balconies on the building, and we were sitting out on the balcony drinking this horrid drink my cousin had given me. I found out later what this stuff was called. I was drinking Cisco, a fruit-flavored wine that was 20 percent alcohol. People called this liquid crack, since it was so easy to drink and it really messed you up. They eventually took it off the market because it was so powerful and could be potentially lethal, with experts stating that a hundred-pound person could die from alcohol poisoning after drinking two bottles in an hour.

The more I drank, the stranger I felt. It was a new experience for me. I ended up getting so inebriated that I walked to the edge of the balcony and climbed up on the railing. My cousin and the others were alarmed.

"Hey, Horse—what are you doing?" Jayden asked.

"I'm Superman," I said as my feet reached the top of the railing.

"Fuck you mean you're Superman?"

It was in the middle of the day, and the open area below us was full of people. Suddenly I had an audience watching me with either amused or concerned faces.

"I'm Superman," I said again. "I can fly!"

I jumped off the balcony, dropping and landing on my feet before falling over. I didn't feel any sort of pain and nothing broke or snapped. I hopped back up on my feet and shouted once more that I was Superman, laughing as I glanced at Jayden. My cousin gave me a look that said, *This fucker is crazy.* I took off running, sprinting across the common area and past kids who looked like they were seeing a ghost. Or maybe a lunatic. I ran like someone possessed, jumping over a fence and racing down the street. When I burst into my house, my mother saw my condition and said my name in a stern tone.

"Andre."

I walked up to her and gave her a defiant "What?" The sort you should never give your mother.

"What?" she repeated, truly shocked by my reply. But I wasn't backing down.

"Yeah—what?"

Steady eyes cut through me as she reached back and slapped me. She slapped me as hard as she could. My mother had never slapped me before, so I stood there stunned. She had whipped me before, but this went to my soul.

"You're not going to do this, not in my house."

I went outside with fury racing through me, and the first thing I could see was a set of plastic chairs outside on our front porch. I struck a chair, punching a big hole through the seat. Feeling dizzy and out of breath, I went back inside to my room and fell onto the bed.

I never drank again. My mother's slap woke me up and warned me of the man I could become if I kept acting like that. Unfortunately, my cousin never got one of those slaps. For a while he was well off and had all these things going for him, but things started to get worse for him. He had a few car wrecks and his father eventually remarried and the new wife disowned him.

Jayden got involved with a lot of bad people. Eventually that bright-eyed and fun-loving guy turned into another kid on the block asking me for a dollar. I remember later on when I was in the military, he asked me if I could help him get some things for his children. Even though it was hard for me since I didn't have a lot of money, I ended up going to Walmart and buying the kids some clothes and tearing up the receipt. That's how much trust I had in Jayden by then.

My relationship with Jayden faded away, as it did with a lot of kids I knew growing up. The rising epidemic of drugs ended up killing a lot of my friends. After going off to the Army, it seemed like every time my mother called, she would tell me about another kid dying. "You know Freddy passed away." "No, Mom, I didn't know." Everybody just started dying. And I'm not going to lie. It made me so sad, because I had to live and go on without them in my life. Over the years, so many of my relationships and friendships died off. And these former friends began to suspect that I felt I was above them.

"You think you're so special, don't you?" I remember one of them saying.

"Yeah, I am special," I said. "But you could be also. This is your choice. You are in the same spot we were in fifteen years ago with the same bottle in your hand doing the same exact thing. Making fun of others and joking but doing nothing with your life."

Sometimes to help somebody else change their life, you have to change yourself. And sometimes that change requires a slap in the face, either figuratively or, in my case, literally.

★   ★   ★

After getting fired from Kmart, my war with my manager was over, but I had a new problem. I was a senior, and high school graduation was approaching. I needed to have a job so I could earn a couple credits. Without those credits, I would have to go to summer school and I wouldn't walk with my fellow classmates at the end-of-the-year ceremony.

I didn't know what to do. It wasn't like there were jobs on every corner for a kid like me. Then I thought of Harden's Superette. I had grown up going to the grocery store, walking there as a little kid with a food stamp in my hand to get some penny candy. The store was named after Mr. Harden. He reminded me of Willie Nelson, the grizzled country singer. Every time I saw him he was smiling. His wife was stiff and mean—that was her cover—but Mr. Harden would always greet me with a loud "Andre!" He had watched me grow up. I decided to tell him about my situation.

"Mr. Harden, I need a job to graduate," I explained to him. "I'll work here absolutely free. Whatever you want me to do, I don't care. I'll do it. I just need it to graduate."

He gave me a nod. "Let me think about it."

A couple of days later, I went into the store to buy something and Mr. Harden saw me.

"Andre! So when are you ready?"

I wasn't sure what he was talking about. "Ready for what?"

"Ready to come to work."

"Sir, I'm ready."

He smiled. "And it's not going to be for free. I'm paying you. And I'm going to work you hard."

"Yes, sir."

I couldn't believe it. I worked at Mr. Harden's store for a few months. From there I went to the military. While I was still in basic, I remember giving my mom a call on a pay phone and hearing the news about Mr. Harden.

"Andre, I have something to tell you," she said in a somber tone. "Mr. Harden passed away."

"What do you mean he passed away?" I said.

Mr. Harden seemed healthy and was only in his fifties. I couldn't believe he was gone.

I never got a chance to thank him.

He was a really nice and genuine man, someone who had given me a chance. Mr. Harden was also family. I remember crying after I heard the news of his passing.

It took me about eight or nine years to finally walk back into that store. The little grocery store felt so small to me, but then again, I had gotten so much bigger. I remember purchasing one of the drinks I used to get, some fruit punch that came in a small carton. They called it fruit punch, but really it was just sugar water. I picked it up and brought it to the counter, where Mrs. Harden checked me out. The woman stood only 4'9" or 4'10", and with her squeaky voice she said, "Will that be all for you?" Her eyes looked up at me behind her glasses.

"Yes, ma'am, that will be all."

As she studied me, she looked astonished. "My, you're a big one."

"Yes, ma'am."

Maybe she recognized my voice or saw something familiar in my eyes.

"Andre? Is that you?"

I smiled and said yes. Without hesitation, she ran around the corner and gave me a hug that lasted a few moments. When I saw her eyes again, they were full of tears.

"I have been following you," she told me. "Charles would be so proud of you."

Remember: they were family. In this little town of black and white and the KKK, this was my family.

★ ★ ★

With my graduation dilemma solved, I looked beyond school and considered my options. I received one college scholarship offer to play football. I got another to run track and a tryout for the Olympics because of my speed in the one hundred meters. On top of those opportunities, I also had a scholarship to an art college.

Yes, I had these opportunities in front of me, but I was always a free thinker. Sometimes I took advice from others, but sometimes I didn't want hear anything but my own thoughts. Most of the time I just wanted to figure things out myself. I tell people now, *Don't do that!* That's why I give advice freely these days, so people don't do like I did and find out the hard way. At the same time, if I had taken anybody's advice, it probably would have been from my brother, who would have wanted me to go into the Navy or the Marines. I don't know what my life would have looked like if I had done that, but I know for a fact I wouldn't be here now. I might be in a better place. I might be a billionaire. Or I might be dead. I don't know and I don't care.

I didn't talk to my father or my brothers or anybody about my decision. I was always a loner, and one day I looked at my scholarships and I decided to just put all of them away and not think about them again. I didn't care about any of them because my mindset was to work. Guys go to work, girls go to school. That's what my father taught me. I knew I didn't want to be poor. I didn't want to go through the struggles that I saw so many people have. It was natural for me to choose the military. I was thinking about the future and I thought about my brothers. One was in the Navy, and my other brother had served as a merchant marine. I thought about how my sisters were teachers who helped others. I wanted to serve my country. At the time, everybody was telling me, "Get your education, get your education," but I had no plans for education. I could have taken one of those scholarships, but I didn't go for that.

Without telling anybody else, I joined the Army.

★ ★ ★

"Hey, Daddy. I have something to tell you."

I called him Daddy sometimes. Not Pops or Papa but Daddy. Maybe it was a sign of endearment, or maybe it was me trying to say, *Hey, be gentle with me this time.*

"What's that, Dre?" he asked as he sat in the familiar old armchair in the family room.

When I saw the look on his face, I knew my mom had already told him. I knew she had. She was the only one I told after joining the Army, and right away she told me I had to tell my father. I asked her why couldn't I simply go and not say anything, but she forced me to tell him the truth. I know Mom wanted me to hear his thoughts.

I sat down across from him. "Well, Dad, I'm going into the military. I joined the Army."

His face didn't change, and his body didn't shift in its seat. Those eyes just looked at me.

"That's what you want to do?"

I gave a nervous nod. "Yeah, that's what I'm doing. I just—I need more. I want to serve. I want to do something with my life."

"Well, you are doing something. You're doing a lot here." His expression revealed no emotion. His countenance appeared as hard as his hands as he spoke. "Your mother's here. I'm here. You got a lot going on here."

"Yes, sir. But I need more."

"Well, if that's what you want," he said. "But when you go, you better go and you better do everything to give it your all. You're going to have to remember this, because it's going to be hard. There's not going to be anybody to hold your hand. There's not going to be anybody taking care of you. And there's going to be a lot of people who don't like you, Dre. They won't like you. They're not going to like you even if they say they like you. But looking at you, they're going to tell you they don't like you because there's nothing you can do about it. There's nothing you'll be able to do about it. Not in the same way me and your mom and everybody else that was here, we dealt with it."

There was no anger in his tone, just an assurance that he was telling me the truth. He no longer spoke to me as a child, but rather as a man.

"You want to go out, Dre? You want to do something that you don't know? You go ahead and do that. You go right ahead. You just make sure that you keep in touch with your family."

"Yes, sir," I replied.

I knew I would keep in touch with my family. After all, I was a mama's boy. The first thing I planned to do every time I had a penny was give it to my mother.

I'm also going to give it my all, I promised myself. *I can take care of myself.*

I had a lot to learn.

IN THE ARMY NOW

An army marches on its stomach.

NAPOLEON

"What's your name, private?!"

The drill sergeant yelling at me didn't really want to know my name. He was singling me out, setting a target on my back. I stood in formation with all of the others for the first time at boot camp as the rain drenched us. We had just stepped off the bus after arriving at Fort Jackson in Columbia, South Carolina. Even though I was eighteen, I knew I looked dominant. Hell—I *was* dominant.

"Private Rush," I called out.

"Private Rush. Can you whip anybody's ass out here?"

"Yes, drill sergeant!" I said without hesitation.

The stern and chiseled face gave no reaction. He simply motioned me to move.

"You get out front," the drill sergeant commanded. "You're in charge."

Oh shit.

I didn't know what he was talking about, what that actually meant. I didn't realize he was making me platoon sergeant after being around me for a few minutes. I also didn't realize that right there and then he was putting a mark on me. Right away he was setting me on a certain path, because instantly I had to deal with all these different people and personalities. I was forced to step out of the shadows and start to become the man I am today.

The place I came from was a black-and-white snapshot called Columbus, Mississippi. When I arrived at Fort Jackson, the picture bled into colors. Right away there was this wonderful collaboration of colors and ethnicities, from yellows and lighter tones to mixtures of dark tans. I had no idea what I was doing at the time, but I soon discovered I had an ability to talk to all sorts of people, to understand them. I went from a straight introvert to an extrovert. *When it's showtime, it's talk time.* Unbeknownst to me, I could do that. I had never been the talker; I was always the shy kid. When I started talking, I had to do the same thing I do now. Being in and out, because there were a lot of alphas and lots of kids with testosterone, so that meant there was a lot of fighting.

Right away, when I got to MEPS (Military Entrance Processing Station), I became disgusted. There wasn't the excitement one might imagine when joining the Army. It was disheartening. Back then, being so young, I felt like I was working at a fast-food place. Nobody fucking cared. Nobody was there to help you or support you or do anything. The people asking questions that determined whether I was fit to serve in the military were impersonal and unwelcoming. The qualifications MEPS determined were physical, mental, and moral. Enduring their questions was a terrible experience.

One of the things they liked to do in MEPS was coerce you into admitting to things you never did, like smoking weed.

"You don't smoke *anything*?" they asked.

"No, I don't," I stated.

"Come on—you know you smoke a little weed."

Most everybody would eventually admit it and say, "Yeah, just a little bit," but I didn't because I was telling the truth.

"But you were around the smoking, right?" they continued. "Did you inhale it?"

"Of course I was around it," I said.

"See—he smoked," they said as they wrote in their report.

I quickly realized I was just another name and another number, yet because of my size, I stood out. At Fort Jackson for basic training, the drill sergeant pulled me out and placed me in a leadership role. Later on, when I got to AIT (advanced individual training), the same thing would happen. By then I had made a name for myself, not in the field but in the kitchen.

★ ★ ★

I believed in the myth that there were absolutely no opportunities for me in Mississippi. My dad's mentality was boys went to work and girls went to school. That was all he knew, having dropped out of elementary school to help his family. I grew up with the desire to not be poor and not have to go through the same struggles so many others did. I assumed the best route to take would be the military, but soon after joining, I realized this wasn't going to be the place where I could become rich or even have any financial stability. So many of the enlisted men in the military struggled their asses off.

I decided to become a cook in the Army because it reminded me of my mother and of how I felt when she cooked. I thought I could do the same thing for the men around me, give them the same sort of feeling every time I helped to prepare a meal.

I was wrong, of course. Cooking in the Army was a whole different thing than my mother's cooking. It was all about mass production. Fast, fast, fast. I did everything and learned nothing, all without an ounce of respect. But I was about to change that.

Sometimes people saw me and my physique working out in the gym or exercising, and they would ask, "What's your MOS?" This stands for military occupational specialties; MOS is what the Army calls its jobs.

"I'm a 94 Bravo," I replied.

"What is that?" they would ask in disbelief. "Is that a cook?"

"Yeah."

"*You're* a cook?"

"What the fuck you say?" I asked, looking them in the eyes.

"Oh, no, no—nothing's wrong with that."

Damn right there's nothing wrong with it. It was easy and common to make fun of the cooks when we worked the hardest and got the least respect. It's the hardest fucking job in the military. It's like hospitality in a restaurant these days. The job was extremely difficult, but people didn't realize that. Once I got there, I was on one side in the kitchen, and I decided that this prevalent attitude was going to fucking change. I didn't know anything. All I knew was Mississippi, and now all I knew was big #10 cans of shit that we fed to everybody.

It takes a true talent to turn the slop from a #10 can into something noticeable. Right away I started doing my own thing, making little twists on the meals. People actually began to ask who cooked this and who made that. I was simply being myself, trying to do the best job I could, even if I could never replicate my mother's home cooking.

★ ★ ★

After joining the Army, I spent time in Fort Stewart, Georgia; 503 Infantry at Camp Casey, Korea; Fort Campbell, Kentucky; and Fort Bragg, North Carolina. It was at Fort Campbell that I felt a rare moment of pride at being recognized for a change. This pride lasted a whole two days.

I was a specialist at the time, an E4, and I had earned that rank. When you first join the Army, you are a private (E1), then get promoted to private second class (E2) and private first class (E3). Becoming a specialist meant I held the same pay grade as a corporal. I worked my ass off, doing so much and always exceeding expectations. When I say I exceeded expectations, that means I led the runs, I led the pushes, and I led the charges. I was always first in everything and always the last to get recognized. That changed when they came to me one day.

"Specialist Rush, you're doing an immaculate job. So much that we are going to give you corporal."

"Really?"

Corporal was in between an E4 and E5, which is a sergeant. Now, Fort Campbell is air assault country, the place where soldiers went to earn their wings. Giving me corporal was like they were saying, "You're better than E4 and you've been exceptional." So I had corporal on for two days.

One day I was in line wearing my corporal stripes, and a sergeant major (the highest enlisted rank) spotted me and then called out, "Corporal Rush." I faced the Hispanic guy and said, "Roger, Sergeant Major." He looked at my new stripes and then said, "Huh—no Air Assault."

"Actually, I'm going to take the next course in two weeks," I replied.

Without saying anything else to me, he walked off. That evening I was called back in and told they were taking my corporal back.

"You have to go back to being a specialist," they told me.

"Why's that?" I asked.

"Because you don't have your Air Assault badge."

I was dumbfounded. "But I'm going to Air Assault."

"So after you come back, you can have your corporal stripes back on."

Now I was angry.

"Woah, wait a second," I began, reminding them of all the things I had been doing in a leadership position. I was at the fucking top of my class, maximizing my push-ups, maxing my PT test. "I'm all over the place. I run circles around the NCOs in here. And you're taking it away from me?"

"Yeah. That's just the way we do it here."

"Fuck you, fuck you, and fuck you. Fuck your dog too. I'm not going to Air Assault. Take your corporal stripe back. I don't give a fuck."

I sure told them. But honestly, I should have gone to Air Assault to earn my badge. But when another man judged me without looking at my background or my profile, it was Mississippi all over again. They were saying that because I didn't have a certain badge I wasn't qualified, but I refused to back down. I wasn't in Columbus anymore, yet I was being judged because I came from Mississippi, and I knew that wasn't right. Sure, this was a thing of pride and a feeling of selfishness, but I was being held back for no reason other than racism and someone being on a power trip. I could deal with not getting accolades and affirmation from all my work, but once again I was being held back. I felt like I was in elementary school again.

A few months after they took off corporal, I put on E5, sergeant. This meant I was above corporal, making more money. I didn't care about the rank or the money, however. When the sergeant major saw me again, he asked, "Where's your wings?" Didn't have them, nor did I intend to earn them.

"I'm not going," I said.

I was urged to go to Air Assault School and earn my wings, but I refused.

"I don't have to go anywhere. I don't have to do anything."

This was my mentality when I started in the military, and it is still my mentality now. Somehow, it's aligned with my values. There are certain principles deep-rooted inside of me, and I abide by them. Sometimes pride will get in the way. I use the word "pride" a lot because back then, people always wanted me to kiss ass. And a guy like me just can't do that. At least not easily. Unless I do it strategically.

★　★　★

Cooking in the Army reinvigorated my exploration of art, but I would come to embrace a new form. It wouldn't involve pen and paper and ink. This art form involved chainsaws and ice.

Before enlisting in the Army, I had never seen an ice carving before. As I've said, the only experience with snow in my childhood resulted in a terrible ear infection, but I'd still loved going out in a snowstorm. So if snow fascinated me, of course I would be blown away when I first saw someone doing an ice carving.

When I was a private, a guy had shown up in our DFAC (Dining facilities Administration Center) with this massive chunk of ice. Suddenly he had a chainsaw growling in his hand and he commenced to slice and trim and cut and smooth the ice until a sculpture emerged. When I saw the wings, I realized it was an eagle. I marveled at how the man had worked his saw to make this creation.

Sometime later, as Thanksgiving approached, I was the youngest cook in this DFAC. One day during a brief, the DFAC manager talked about the upcoming holiday and asked if anybody there knew how to do an ice carving. Without thinking, I said, "Me!" I didn't even realize I had raised my hand.

"Private Rush! You know how to do ice carving?"

"Yes, sergeant."

I had no idea.

He accepted me at my word and then told me the details, what he was going to do and where I would go and what he wanted. All I said was "Yes, sir." After the meeting, my friends came around me asking if I could do an ice carving.

"We'll find out," I said.

Of course I was shitting bricks. They drove me over in a van and dropped me off at TISA (Troop Issue Subsistence Activities). TISA was the place that handled all the logistics of providing the food and equipment for dining facilities. I didn't know what I needed, so I simply told them I was there to do an ice carving. The technician told me it was in a freezer and said he would bring it out for me. Moments later, two mammoth, 350-pound blocks of ice stood in front of me. They were inside of cardboard boxes with plastic underneath. A chainsaw had been brought out as well.

For fifteen minutes, I just stared at the ice and the chainsaw, wondering how the hell to even begin. Finally I went to one of the guys there and asked if he could start the chainsaw for me. I wasn't exactly sure how. I had seen them before in Mississippi but had never actually used one. Once I held the chainsaw in my hands, I remembered the guy I had seen making that sculpture. I had paused that performance, so all I did was start replaying it in mind and enacting his performance. I just continued to do what I had seen him doing. I was hesitant when the moving blade first touched the ice. I tapped it to see what happened, then began messing around with it and playing.

For the first block of ice, I sculpted a cornucopia, the big, horn-shaped basket overflowing with fruit and vegetables. But that wasn't the difficult one. I also decided to make a bald eagle. For four and a half hours I worked on these enormous ice blocks, chiseling and carving and looking and studying, all while I circled them. When I finally got done, it was wet and dripping everywhere because it was tempered. They put the sculptures back in the freezer and I left, unsure of how my carvings looked.

The next day, on Thanksgiving, they brought out the ice sculptures, and everybody came to see them. We'd never gotten ice carvings before, so this was a big deal. The DFAC manager pulled off the covering to display the cornucopia and the bald eagle. I could hear the sound of surprise and admiration in the DFAC.

"Private Rush. You did this?"

"Yes, sergeant. I did that."

He examined the sculptures and nodded. "It's a damn good job."

"I know," I replied, thinking, *Shit, I don't know how to do this.*

When I think about those two pieces now, they were fine for a beginner, but they still were so messy and amateurish. But it was better than anybody else had done. I used my artistic skills on a piece of ice. Eventually I would be doing the same thing with chocolate and sugar and beeswax (which is basically fat) and all sorts of other primaries. And I did this all from visualizing the piece in my head and working it out. I never illustrated anything before I started carving. I didn't even realize this was unusual until a little later, during a competition, when a professional sculptor came up to me and asked what I was going to carve.

I came to learn that teams of professionals had been participating in ice-carving competitions for years. One seasoned veteran saw me at this competition and wanted to know what I was planning to make.

"I don't know," I admitted.

The competition was getting ready to start and I had five blocks of ice in front of me. This man had sketched out all he was doing with his carvings.

"You don't have to be like that," the guy said to me.

"I don't understand. What do you mean?"

"If you don't want to share what you're doing, you don't have to share."

I shook my head. "No. I honestly do not know."

When the competition began, this man was next to me with a group of assistants along with all this equipment like Dremel rotary tools and plans and diagrams all laid out on the floor. All I had was my chainsaw, one Dremel tool, and a few wood chisels, because I couldn't afford real ones. I started to cut out an eagle attacking a snake that surrounded him. While I was doing this, the man next to me kept looking over, seeing what I was doing. He eventually realized I wasn't lying to him. As I carved, I spoke out loud. "Maybe I'll do an eagle," I said, and then I'd say that was not enough, that I needed to do a snake, talking to myself as I continued to carve. "I'm going to put wings on the snake and make him a flying snake," I said and proceeded to do this.

After the competition was finished, the guy came up to me with a whole different demeanor.

"That was fucking incredible," he said. "I want you to carve with me. Let's team up."

"All right," I said.

He was an excellent ice carver, and we did end up teaming up and competing together.

I would have never even started competing if it wasn't for those first Thanksgiving ice sculptures I made. A sergeant major who saw those sculptures wanted to know who carved them, and that's when I was asked to be on the culinary team. When I first heard this, I had no idea what the word "culinary" even meant. I just cooked. I didn't know there was such a thing as culinary competitions, or that there were huge contests where everybody cooked everything on a professional scale. This sergeant major brought me in the first time and introduced me to the culinary team who had been there for a few years. Now I was with experts who knew what they were doing. I was young and had never done any of this before. These guys could teach me.

Of course, that's what I wanted and wished for. But it never seems to happen that way.

One of the team leaders had been participating in these culinary competitions for twelve or thirteen years. He was a cake guy and I loved pastries. The sergeant major assigned him to train me, so I accompanied him and watched as he worked on these creatively decorated cakes. What he was doing was so boring, but I studied what he did. One day while he was away, I came in and saw a cake this guy had made. I decided to make one myself, knowing enough of what he had done to make one.

Back in those days, they used fruitcakes for the base of decorative display cakes (like the kind used in culinary competitions) because they were very dense and held their shape well. This was the foundation. We made royal icing that hardened to a porcelain-like texture, creating such a smooth surface it didn't appear real. After we put the royal icing around the cake, we used sandpaper to scrub off the edges and piping tips to create special motifs. Flowers were made out of fondant and gum paste.

I had seen this guy doing all these things, so I replicated his actions and added my own artistic flair to them. There I was, this young black guy from Mississippi working on a fruitcake, and I felt a sense of pride in my abilities. *Hey, I think I'm onto something.* I knew I was good at this. When the team leader who had been showing me how to bake came back the next day, he saw my cake next to his and wanted to know who did this. I told him it was me, and his reaction was the opposite of what I'd imagined it would be.

"Oh, hell no," he said. "I'm done. I'm not showing you anything else. You're learning too fast."

Then he walked away

I laughed and said, "Okay," believing he was just messing with me, but he didn't come back. He meant those words. I thought, *What the hell?* He never taught me anything else again. This wasn't the first time something like that happened, and it certainly wouldn't be the last. But that didn't matter.

You don't have to teach me. If I see it done, it's mine. I'm going to get it and then I'm going to make it better.

That was always my motto.

In my first competition, I used my skills to paint an elaborate angel on a plate I made out of pastillage (hard sugar). I used cocoa food coloring as my paint, and my work made such an impression that I ended up on the front page of *Fort Lee Traveller,* the local newspaper for Fort Lee, Virginia, and the Fort Lee base, which was the quartermaster school for all the cooks. Not only was I pictured on the cover, but it was the first time our base had been featured after being in hundreds of competitions. The sergeant major was so proud to see a private like me doing that. This is what solidified my competing in culinary competitions, and that happened during my first year.

Going to that first competition allowed me to enter a new world. I saw everything that the culinary craft offered. I heard everybody calling each other chef. *Chef.* That's what I wanted to be called. They were still calling me a cook, and that's what I was. I wasn't a chef; I was just a cook. And every time I left for a competition and came back to my combat unit, my commander or anybody else would look at me with an attitude of "Okay, that's enough of that cooking shit. Now it's time for us to get back to the *real* military."

Nobody was showing me how to excel in my culinary art. Hell, nobody around me knew anything about this, so I had to figure it all out on my own. This was before I could go online and google information on it. There was no Instagram or Pinterest. I went out and bought books on cooking that I couldn't have afforded as a private. Most of the time there weren't even color photos I could learn from. Ultimately, my education came from doing the work myself at the culinary competitions, which in reality only added up to two weeks a year. I decided to make every single competition count.

Back then, you could enter whatever cooking competition you wanted, but you couldn't enter too many because of how much work was involved with each contest. We would stay up all night putting things together. By my fourth competition at Fort Lee, I wanted to soak up as many experiences as I could, so I entered as many competitions as possible. I didn't have any of the tools or equipment to practice on throughout the year, so I always picked up where I left off. Some guys would do two or three different categories, but I wanted to compete, so I entered fifteen contests that year. Unfucking heard of. I was a young guy. I could do it. For the next week and a half, I worked my ass off, twenty-four hours a day, just rushing and creating and baking. I loved it.

When it came time to cross the stage because you won a gold, silver, bronze, or commendable, or maybe you didn't win anything, I started to get my name called again and again. One medal. Two. Three. Four. Ten. Fifteen. They kept giving them to me, and at the end the guy handing out the medals joked with me. "It's a good thing you're a big guy, because that's a lot of medals around your neck. You can carry them." He didn't understand that this had nothing to do with those medals. I didn't care about them. It was all about the experience. I needed this time cooking and baking. Experience is the best teacher for me, and I didn't have the opportunity to learn except like this. People thought my victories were about clout or winning. They didn't understand it was about passion.

They didn't understand the prevailing attitude deep inside of me.

If I'm going to be here and do this, I'm going to do it 100 percent completely.

That was how I learned my culinary arts. Just by doing it and doing it and doing it.

★ ★ ★

Some people noticed my abilities and attitude. One day I received a call from someone.

"Sergeant. I think I got a job you might want. What do you think about going to DC?"

"What?" I asked. "Why go to DC?"

"You want to go to the Pentagon?"

"The Pentagon? Do you need me to take someone out?"

"No, Sergeant. Just go there to do what you're good at: cooking. But it's something you have to try out for."

A CAKE FOR THE OCCASION

Oh, I see, so the white man give you a couple a
stripes, and suddenly you start hollerin' and orderin'
everybody around, like you the massa himself!
Nigger, you ain't nothin' but the white man's dog!

DENZEL WASHINGTON IN *GLORY* (1989)

What am I doing here in DC?

I had just stepped off a plane and arrived at the Pentagon to try out for the chairman of the Joint Chiefs of Staff's dining facility. I'm young, black, and in the combat arms unit, and suddenly I'm surrounded by all white chefs from Army, Navy, Air Force, and Marines. None of them were wearing uniforms; most wore polos underneath chef jackets. I didn't wear a chef jacket, so it made me stand out even more. Four others were also trying out for the job. For four days I worked like a dog trying to prove that I was the best person for the job. The other three were there for thirty days.

A great culinary chef and ranger named Dave helped me while I was there, and he was just what I needed. I had done virtually everything in those four days. I had even done an ice carving.

Right before I got back on the plane to my base, someone said they needed one made, so I was carving ice with Dave on the mezzanine. I left the Pentagon drenched from all the ice shavings, and when I sat down on the plane I realized I was soaking wet. Before I left, Dave told me I had done a great job.

Once again, when I arrived back at Fort Campbell, my commander was annoyed that I had been gone.

"Enough of that cook shit," he belted out. "Get back to work."

My commander was a young, arrogant, and pompous prick. You could tell he came from privilege by the entitled way he acted. I could smell it. He had no familiarity with 99 percent of us, but there he was in charge because of placement.

One week passed and I began to wonder. A second week went by, and I grew annoyed. I thought, *Oh well.* By the third week of not hearing anything, I didn't want to waste any more energy thinking about it.

Fuck it. I didn't get it. That's life.

But the fourth week I got a phone call. It was a head chef in the Army who participated in all the competitions and cooked for some of the most important people around. He was badass and someone I respected.

"Chef, we are putting you on orders to come here," he said.

Fuck, yeah, I thought. *Finally something.*

Of course, in my life, nothing has ever been simple and easy. When the order went up to my commander, he erupted.

"Fuck that shit, you're not going there," he told me.

The first thing you come to understand when you enter the military is the importance of rank. Everything is run through the engine of a person's rank. My commander was a major. My battalion commander, however, was a full-bird colonel, and he ended up hearing about me and my situation. He decided to intervene.

"Sergeant Rush is going to DC," the colonel told my commander. "You're going to leave him the fuck alone so he can go."

Before I left, my commander called me in with the first sergeant. My commander was a white guy while the first sergeant was black. I was an E5, still young and still aggressive. The commander stood directly in front of me and scowled at me.

"I understand you're going to DC." His tone was laced with disdain. "You know—you may make it. You might be promoted. You might work there for a while. But you're not going to make it in the long run."

He continued to come at me with insults and hate. Then he delivered the main reason I was there.

"I'm giving you a reprimand," the commander said as he gave me the slip of paper.

This was ridiculous, since a reprimand is only there on your record until you leave, and then it gets torn up. The only reason he was giving me this was because he was upset that he couldn't make me stay.

I smirked and looked at him. "Do you want me to tear it up now or later?"

"Sergeant Rush!" the first sergeant shouted.

"It's a question," I said. "I'll tear it up now."

I ripped the slip in half and walked out of his office. I left and got on a plane headed to DC shortly after that.

Thirteen years later, I ended up seeing the colonel who had ordered my commander to leave me alone. He was now a lieutenant general. The lieutenant general actually remembered me. He was a three-star general now and said he followed what I was doing. The general explained to me why he had helped me. Even though he was a black man, color had nothing to do with his decision.

"We need greatness in the military," the general said. "I knew you would be great."

★　★　★

For the first four years after entering the Army, I had endured an onslaught of hostility, from the alphas who wanted to show me who was boss to those who couldn't see past the color of my skin. I went through a hell of a lot of racial division. It's not like I saw it every day, but sometimes people might think there's not any of that in the military. Racism reared its ugly head time and time again.

After my time at Fort Jackson, Fort Lee, and Fort Stewart, I was stationed in the 503 Infantry at Camp Casey, Korea. During this time, there was some little kid who was openly hostile toward blacks. Nobody liked him. The PFC (private first class) was from some tiny town that was still stuck back in the Civil War. The little kid had a big mouth, and he spewed shit all the time. The DFAC manager at the base who was an SFC (sergeant first class) also happened to be black. One day the little kid called the SFC a nigger while we were in his office. The SFC looked at me and then said, "Bro, close the door." I wasn't sure what he wanted.

"Close the door?"

I shut the door, and the SFC walked over, grabbed the young kid, and threw him against the wall. Even though he wanted to, the SFC didn't hit him, because he knew he couldn't. The kid began wailing and ran out of the office. Naturally, he went and told the IG (Inspector General) on the SFC.

When the IG came and asked what happened, the SFC said he didn't know what the little guy was talking about.

"Specialist Rush was there," the SFC stated.

"I didn't see anything," I said.

Actually, what I saw was a little pissant racist finally getting his head screwed on straight.

Things were like that. It didn't matter about the year or the place or the profession. This sort of hate had been around for a long time, and unfortunately it never seems to go away.

Once, right after I became an E5 (sergeant), I was put in charge when our E7 (SFC) left to retire. To put this in perspective, I had around five years of experience in the military while this E7 had over eighteen years. A lot of people didn't like that I was temporarily in charge, including a master sergeant who was an E8 and Food Service Advisor. This man had been in the military for twenty-eight years, and he was over everything. He was a white guy from Mississippi, and he knew that I had come from there too. I could tell he didn't like me from the very beginning. He treated me like the manager at Kmart had treated me. He would always say smug things to me. It didn't matter how hard I worked; I had busted my ass when I was an E1, then an E2, all the way to making E5. I worked so hard that people put me in charge. This master sergeant couldn't care less about my work ethic.

"I don't speak to E5s," he once said, then added with disdain, "I don't speak to *boys.*"

Everything you needed to know about this guy's character came in the way he said that last word, "boys." This E8 constantly talked down to me, belittling me without me being able to stop him.

One day we were in the dining facility, I was with another E8, a black guy who was much older and had been in the military for more than thirty years. He had told me to stay clear of the racist from Mississippi. While we were there, the master sergeant walked in front of the other E8 and began berating me. This time I didn't hold back on him. I got in his face and spoke my words slowly and carefully.

"If you talk to me like I'm a nigger again, I am going to beat the fuck out of you," I said.

Instantly, he yelled out, "You're threatening me, you're threatening me!" The way cowards do, hiding behind his rank to save whatever pride he might have. The black E8 standing there looked at us with his eyes wide open in surprise, then quickly exited the facility. I knew exactly what was going to happen next. Sure enough, the E8 from Mississippi tried to take this up to get me busted. He stated that I threatened his life, and he wanted the fellow E8 to validate what happened.

"I never heard anything," the islander said. "I didn't hear him say that."

This gentleman who had been in the military for three decades put his career on the line for me. He told me later that he knew how I felt, that he had spent thirty years dealing with shit like that. I was fortunate to not get into trouble. I knew if I had, that would have been the end of my military career. I knew that even as I stood up to the E8, but I was fed up. I had grown so used to the verbal assaults and the dismissive attitudes. This was the norm to me, and it was toxic. I didn't regret confronting him a bit.

After this happened, the E8 never said anything else to me. We both knew what happened. He had just wanted to show he was in charge. I knew it was personal because we were both from Mississippi, so he knew the pecking order. This was a long time ago. The kind of town this master sergeant was from had this prevailing mentality handed down over the generations.

Time and time again, I would be put into situations like this. People would learn they could only push me so far before I pushed back.

★   ★   ★

When I went to DC and started working in the Pentagon, I realized that it was a whole different world. I was coming from the field. I grew up spending time working outdoors on the farm, so I loved the mud and the dirt of Army life. It was a sanctuary for me, even though I was doing so much cooking. I still needed to pound the ground and grit through the physical toil of each day. I remember one time I got into a fight with a boar in the woods because it had come into my tent. Stuff like this was exhilarating. All of that changed when I went to the Pentagon and started working for the chairman of the Joint Chiefs of Staff.

My first week there, I had to come into work early. My uniform looked like a monkey suit with its black pants and white shirt. I was opening up that morning and I felt so nervous about everything. When I went to make the coffee in the big carafe they had, the thing wasn't working for some reason. So naturally I did what any soldier would do: I buddy fucked it. Meaning I made the coffee from scratch. When you're out in the field, you do what you have to do. We don't have filters, so we have to sift the grounds to make coffee. That's exactly what I did.

Shortly after I made the coffee, the master chef, who called me Big Guns Arm & Hammer, came rushing into the kitchen in a state of panic.

"Big Guns! What happened?"

"What are you talking about?" I asked.

"The coffee!"

I shrugged. "It wasn't working, so I had to buddy fuck it."

"I got a complaint about it from the general."

"What?" I couldn't believe it.

"You know we have Starbucks here," he explained to me, telling me I should have done this and that to get good coffee. At that time, I thought to myself, *Motherfucking bitches, these guys are spoiled.* This general in the military, tough as fucking nails, is complaining about some coffee. I refused to take responsibility.

"It wasn't my fault the carafe wasn't working," I said. "I'd drink the coffee I made. It tastes fine."

"Big Guns—they're not like that here."

This was when I began to realize that there was a different attitude here in the Pentagon.

Once again I ran into a master sergeant who was a great chef but who didn't want to show me shit. This head chef was partial to the females, but he treated me like I didn't belong there. He wanted my utmost respect, meaning he wanted me to kiss his ass. I admired him, but I couldn't and wouldn't do this. He had no idea what I'd been through; to this NCO, I was just a kid who was black. But I knew he wasn't a racist because of how he spoke to the girls, many of whom were black, all the time. He wasn't racist; he wasn't interested in helping me out.

One day before we had an event, I went to this chef and I told him the same thing I had told so many others.

"Chef, I'm sorry," I said. "I'm not kissing your ass. Either you're going to show me or I'm going to see it. We're in the same kitchen. That's no disrespect, but I am not kissing anyone's ass for information. I'm just doing my job."

The top chef looked at me with a blank face and said nothing. He never did show me big things, but I watched him long enough to see everything I needed to see.

For instance, we once had this big event for the chairman, which involved royalty. We would be doing the dessert course, and the master sergeant planned on making a cake that he had prepared a million times. It was called the puzzle cake, and it was very intricate and particular. I had seen him making this when he was teaching someone else in the kitchen. The four layers consisted of a chocolate cake, a yellow cake, a white cake, and another chocolate. In between those layers were praline cream, buttercream, and ganache. You baked these layers and then put them in the freezer to harden, almost to the point of being frozen. Then you went around the cake with a long and pointy knife, cutting one inch from the edge and making a ninety-degree angle all the way around. What comes out is a perfect pyramid and a hole in the cake that's about one inch in diameter. You had to turn the pyramid upside down to the tip, then go back to the little round hole on the top of the cake and squash it to the point that it seems like it's going to tear apart. But it doesn't. You fill up the hole with ganache and creams to keep it steadfast in those pockets. Finally you cover it all up with more ganache and buttercream that can be piped around and made really pretty.

All of this results in a cake that provides a delightful surprise when you cut into it. People discover this intricate cake and wonder how we created all these pieces that go up and down and around. When you do this right, you make a cake that's very sexy and beautiful, appropriate for a grand occasion. If you mess up one little part of the puzzle cake, however, you're basically screwed.

On the day of the event with royalty, Chef pulled the puzzle cake out of the fridge, and when the master chef started to cut it, the cake fell apart. He looked aghast as he fell into pure panic mode and looked at the rest of us as if he were drowning. Then Master Chief (the Navy supervisor in charge of the master chef) began cussing like a sailor.

"What the fuck are we going to do now?" he shouted out, his whole morale broken.

There was nothing we could fucking do. We had less than thirty minutes to have this dessert out, and the master chef had to throw it out because he couldn't cut it.

You have to understand that food is the highest of the high. I've said this truth many times before: food has stopped wars and started wars and made treaties. People don't understand how important food is in history. This was one of those moments in time when it wasn't just about a cake we were making. This was about the connection and the experience, about politics and personalities, about an event recorded and an evening remembered. So when the cake suddenly disintegrated, the master chief looked at me with desperation.

"Big Dog. Can you fix this?"

Without hesitation, I said, "Roger, Master Chief."

"Then fix it!" he barked back at me.

This is where preparation can eclipse panic, and where memory can make up for mishaps. Every flash in my brain started firing. The first thing I did was run out of the kitchen and down to the concourse to the bakery that I knew was there. They had sheet cakes, so I begged to buy four of them.

"We don't sell the entire sheet cake," the manager told me.

I wouldn't take no for an answer, and I continued to plead with him. Thankfully they gave them to me, so I ran back upstairs carrying all four of the sheet cakes. I put on chocolate and some heavy cream. Some whipped cream. Some praline cream. I'm doing all this shit in warp time, and meanwhile the head chef who'd fucked up just walked out. This wasn't how he operated. He wasn't a pressure guy. I thrived under pressure. It was like a cooking show, but no cameras were filming me. Ten minutes left. Then seven. Six minutes remaining. I slowed things down, taking each task one at a time. In the final minute the cake was finished.

When I cut the cake, it came out perfect. When the master chef finally saw it, the look on his face was one of humility. It was the first time he ever came over to me to say, "Great job, Chef." I simply said, "Of course, you taught me well." And he had, actually; if I hadn't seen him doing this cake, I wouldn't have known how. After the event was over, the master chief, came up to the master sergeant and reamed him out.

"Chef Rush saved your fucking job," the master chief said to the head chef.

The head chef looked utterly defeated. If only he knew that this wasn't what I wanted. I didn't want some victory over him. I wanted him to look proud.

The story didn't end with the puzzle cake. This chef, who as I said was a badass, ended up becoming my mentor, so much so that he was the one who got me to the White House. He was the one who said, "I'm going to bring you to the door. It's your choice to know how to get in." He got me over to knock on the door at the White House. I got in and I stayed in. When I got there, I didn't look at the pictures or study the scenery. I walked in and asked, "What do I need to do?" That's always been my mentality.

After the incident with the puzzle cake, the master chief gave me some more background information.

"That guy was the one who didn't want you to come here," the master chief told me. "He said you didn't belong."

I knew that before I helped him. Eventually, the master chief himself confessed to this when we started doing competitions together.

"I'm sorry," he said to me. "It wasn't that you weren't talented. I was afraid. You came in, you're new, you're fresh. You're alive. I didn't want to be the person suddenly out of a job."

I looked at him and shook my head. "Chef, don't you understand? I'm here to make *you* look good. I don't care about any of this shit. I don't care about fucking accolades. I'm here to make *you* look good."

★ ★ ★

The moment I'd stepped off the bus at Fort Jackson, people saw me as a big black guy who was intimidating. I couldn't always change attitudes or correct assumptions. As an enlisted, I had to figure out everything myself, especially when it came to being in the kitchen. I needed to learn a lot on my own. Nobody—*nobody*—would help. And not everybody wanted to obey this big, black, intimidating man when he began to give orders. A lot of the guys had gone to culinary school, so they looked down on me, thinking I was trying to take what they had. They rarely offered assistance and information. What they didn't realize was that I was a fly on the wall. They counted me out when they refused to help me. I stayed true to myself, and this was how I succeeded.

When you count me out, you discredit my mindset, you discredit my drive, you discredit my ability to succeed, you discredit my resiliency and my passion.

Everything that others did to discredit me only fueled me as I grew. I sat back and listened and learned. I watched everybody. I watched the good, I watched the bad, and I watched the indifferent. And I learned from each and every last one of them.

All of those who discredited me I took and put in my pocket to save for a later date. That's how Chef Rush came to be born and how he is so successful. If you're going to judge me based on what you see, then you're never going to be able to see everything I can do. That's why I do it by myself. I'm the hardest fucking worker. I'm the most resilient.

It doesn't matter where you come from. You can do anything if you're willing to work for it.

GIVE ME ALL YOUR MONEY

Money won't create success,
the freedom to make it will.

NELSON MANDELA

For the first few years after moving to DC, I let cooking consume me. The culinary world does that to people, whether it's through tyrannical chefs who crush your confidence or through the tough conditions cooking can entail. Neither of these were deterrents for me. In addition to working at the Pentagon, I was studying hotel and restaurant management, taking classes at culinary school, and teaching and training others. I was also doing catering jobs on the side. The catering jobs were the killers because they sometimes kept me out until two in the morning and I was so wired at the end of the job, it was hard to sleep.

The event confirming that I needed to make a change and go out on my own happened with one of the catering companies I worked for. This caterer was the most prominent in the DC area, which meant they had to hire lots of people and had high employee turnover. They didn't pay well, but it was more than I made, and they didn't always hire people with experience. For this particular large event, we were providing French banquet service, where platters of food were assembled in the kitchen and then served to guests at their table à la carte. Two servers usually worked together with a round table of ten. This service required a lot of skill, since you needed to hold the tray of food with one hand and then serve people individually with two wooden utensils in your other hand.

Most of the time, because I enjoyed the hectic pace, I did both the front and the back of the house for an event. The front involved service while the back involved cooking. For this event, I happened to be working at the front of the house. I knew I wanted to strike out on my own, and this would provide me with more experience.

As I was serving one table, I noticed a young and petite female from another country who was working at the table next to me. She looked like she probably weighed no more than ninety pounds and was at most 4'9". She was new, and I could tell she was struggling to balance her tray with one hand. The manager saw her struggling, too, so he went over to her and aggressively snatched the tray from her right in front of the guests.

"Get out of here," he ordered.

The young lady began to cry and scampered away. Watching all of this unfold right in front of me triggered me in a bad way. Soon after finishing serving the table, I noticed the manager walking to the back of the hall, so I decided to follow him. The kitchen was busy and alive with energy and movement. As the man in charge noticed me behind him, he stopped and gave me a dismissive look.

"What's your problem?" he said as half a dozen different chefs worked around us.

"If you ever do that again, I'll break your hand," I told him.

He just stared, processing what I'd just said amidst the noise of clanking dishes and grilling meat. The manager looked incredulous.

"No, I'm serious," I said with force. "If you ever fucking snatch something out of somebody else's hand in front of me again, I will break your hand. Especially if you do it to a female. She was doing her best."

I waited for a response, but he didn't say a word. Of course, he had a few words to say to others about me. When I found the girl later, she was bawling, so I tried to console her.

"It's okay," I said. "You need to find something else to do. You should never be humiliated by someone like that."

I understood that she needed the work, but at the same time she needed her self-respect even more. When the event was finished, one of my colleagues came to me and told me that I couldn't say things like that, not to the manager.

"Don't worry. I'm not going to say anything again because I'm not going to be here anymore."

I was making great money, but I was killing myself. Sleeping two or three hours a night, working nonstop, and dealing with shit like this.

Something has to change.

I was a young kid in DC, working all these jobs and now making around fifty dollars an hour, which for me was big money. It was huge. I was pushing myself not just because I enjoyed working so much, but because I knew I could do so many things to earn money. I wasn't making it to spend it but to save it. However, as I said, I was young, and I started doing the same thing every other black person usually does, putting all the money in a stupid-ass bank with no interest or money market accounts or anything. Income was finally coming in, but I wasn't being smart with it since I didn't know how to be. I was asking people around me who had the means, inquiring about things like stocks and investments, but I got absolutely fucking nothing. As usual, no one helped me. So instead of easing up on my workload and quitting the catering business, I decided I would start my own.

One morning I strode into the Pentagon kitchen and made my announcement.

"Who wants to start a business with me?"

Cue the sound of crickets in the background.

I knew I wasn't the most popular guy in the kitchen, thanks to my crazy work ethic and my big damn mouth. I also happened to be the only black guy on staff. These guys were seasoned chefs who had been there a long time, and there I was this young kid coming in with excitement and dreams saying, "Hey! I'm just doing my own catering company. Who's down? Who's with me?" The silence was followed with a "Shut up" and a "What are you talking about" as everyone turned and went back to work.

Fuck y'all, I thought. *I'll do it myself.*

A few days later, the phone rang in the Pentagon kitchen. I answered, and a man's voice said, "I'm looking for a caterer."

"You just found one," I replied.

It actually was a common thing for someone to be calling the Pentagon looking for a caterer. People in the Washington area knew that all the chefs at the Pentagon were exceptionally well trained and highly vetted. Pentagon chefs also had security clearance, so they could be trusted in wealthy people's homes. A lot of us were known to do side jobs, so the Pentagon was a great culinary resource.

I had a phone meeting with the couple that was hosting the party, and it went well. They told me the kind of event they were hosting, a dinner party for about twenty guests. I made some suggestions about the menu and presentation, and we chatted back and forth. They liked me; I liked them. The only thing we didn't talk about was my fee. I was new to the business side of catering, and I was a little shy about the topic. They didn't ask about the money, and I didn't bring it up. I got the job.

The day of the event, I drove to the clients' house. It was in Virginia, a pretty long haul from DC. As I steered through their gates onto the longest driveway I'd ever seen in my life and arrived at the house, I stared in astonishment.

Holy crap.

It was like looking at the Matterhorn for the first time. I later found out that the man of the house was the head of one of the major tech giants of that era, and the woman was a well-known writer and cancer survivor. I wasn't exactly intimidated by the setting—I'd been working at 1600 Pennsylvania Avenue, after all—but I knew I would need to be on top of my game.

As I climbed out of my car, I walked to the front door. I was the only cook coming. Nobody had wanted to help me, so that meant I did the shopping and would end up doing all the prep and cooking and cleanup. I didn't care; I just needed to know what they needed. When I went into the house and began to set up for the event, I met the family. The woman and her husband were a really nice couple with daughters.

I worked my ass off—as I always do—throughout the late afternoon and evening. When you're doing a private catering gig, you've got to be in it 120 percent, from beginning to end. There are so many details you need to get right, there's no time to do anything but focus, focus, focus. Full presence. Full commitment. Time flies, and when you're finished with the job, you can barely stand on your feet.

After the party was over, the lady of the house came up to me and said, "Andre, I loved it, loved it, loved everything. You did a masterful job. So what do we owe you?"

Here it was, the moment of truth. I'd spent about five or six hundred dollars on ingredients and supplies, so I was thinking of asking maybe double that. I knew that might be pushing it, but I did have to factor in travel time and prep and planning and shopping. So I went for it.

"Ma'am, I'm not going to lie to you. I don't even know. I just started this business and all I can do is tell you what I paid for food, which was around seven hundred bucks. How does twelve hundred sound?"

She looked at me and smiled, then said, "Stay right there."

Is that too much? I wondered as she went upstairs. *Is she getting her husband to negotiate?* When she came back down, she was holding a checkbook and a hardcover book. The book was one she had written—a motivational/inspirational title. She scribbled an inscription on the first page and filled out the check. Then she slipped the check inside the book and handed it to me. Guess she'd decided to give me my full asking price after all.

"I have only one piece of advice for you, Andre," she said. "Know your worth."

I figured she was castigating me for my fee, but she seemed to be in a good mood as she and her husband walked me out. I got into my car and, as soon as they left, I breathed a sigh of relief. I had just completed my first job as an independent caterer, it had gone well, I had a check in my hand, and I was feeling pretty chill. At least I was until I opened the book and pulled out the check. For a moment I thought there had to be some mistake.

Pay to the Order of Andre Rush: Eight Thousand Dollars.

My heart damn near ripped itself out of my chest. This was mind-blowing. That check didn't just change the way I thought of my value as a chef; it literally changed my life. My attitude changed instantly, as immediately as a switch turning on a light. When I heard her words and read that check, suddenly I knew

I could never undervalue my worth—that I was my biggest asset. Everything now was a game changer. Every event I catered and every person I cooked for. They all mattered because I knew *I* mattered.

★   ★   ★

Just like that, things began to open up for me and my catering business. It felt like watching a wildfire start to blaze. I was a pastry chef, so I started doing all sorts of cakes—half cakes going out the door like crazy at $75, full sheets at $150 a pop. My busyness only grew as I kept going—moving and connecting and pushing. Doing lots of little crazy, fun things for VIPs. People asking for me by name even though they didn't know what I looked like. All these experiences taught me to know more not just about this business but about myself. I began to figure out what was acceptable, what I needed to refrain from, what the temperature of a room felt like, what mattered the most to my customers. I told myself, *You have to think about who you are, what you are, and how you are.*

Back then, I was a young black guy who was very talented, ambitious, and driven. I was a hard worker, but sometimes I was not the person who should have been out front. I understood the dynamics of certain events, so for some of them I hired a white female who could talk for me, while I attended as if I were the help. This wasn't something hard for me to do; this was me being smart. No matter if I was dressed up or down, people were still going to get a first impression of me. I needed them to respect me regardless. I have gotten jobs because of the way I look and I have lost jobs for the same reason.

My whole life has been spent being noticed even when I didn't want to be. There was an equation that I could always count on: Being Noticed + Success = Getting Hate. Because I was so busy at this time, word got back to the branch. The branch are the people who control where you go in the military, and the branch manager called me up. I soon discovered he was talking shit about me because he heard I was doing so much. He also happened to be a black guy. People told me, "Watch out for this guy." He ended up trying to get me out of DC. This guy knew what I was doing, so he was trying to take over and get this for himself. Eventually I got him on the phone to ask him what he was doing.

"I need to see you off to better your career," he said.

"Better my career? I'm the same fucking rank as you. And why do you give a fuck about my career?"

He made excuses now that he was talking to the real person instead of a name and figure he had only heard about and resented. I didn't want to hear any of them.

"Okay, I'll make you a deal," I said. "I'll go wherever you want me to go if you whip my ass. If I whip your ass, you just shut the fuck up."

Of course, I was being sarcastic because there was no chance that would ever happen in the first place. That was how I dealt with things like this. That was the nature of the beast, just human nature, which was fine with me. Some people want to piggyback off others. I wasn't about to let that happen.

★ ★ ★

As I've said, one of the biggest reasons for entering the Army was because I didn't see other future prospects, and once I started serving in the military, I also began to save money. I needed to do whatever I could do to secure a better future for myself and help my mother and my family. I always had this mindset; even when I was in high school, I worked and gave most of my money to my mom. Before I left my job with Mr. Harden and joined the Army, I told myself there were two things I needed to do. The first was to set myself up with a line of credit and the second was to start a savings account. I ended up surprising all my friends and family members when I did both.

Right before I went to Korea, I went to a small bank in Mississippi and told them I needed a credit line. To do that, I ended up buying something for $1,500. It was the first and last unnecessary luxury item I would ever purchase. Actually, there were four items I bought: fancy rims for a car I didn't have yet. This was me making a promise to myself that one day I would buy a car, something I never had in school (and no, I'm not counting that piece-of-junk Buick I had to borrow money for only to see it explode!).

Since this was one of those mom-and-pop banks and not a national one, I asked a family member I won't name to help me out, since I was going to be out of the country and wouldn't be able to make transactions or check on things. I explained how every month I was putting $500 out of the $700 I earned into this bank account to save for the future, and I needed someone to pay off my $1,500 car rims to help me build my credit. When I left for Korea, I had this set up and didn't worry another minute about it. This was how I was saving for retirement. *That* was the extent of my plans as far as financial investments were concerned. I didn't know anything except that I knew people spent their money once they earned it, so I simply decided to save as much as I could.

Several years later, during my busy catering days, I finally allowed myself to buy something using some of the money I had made. I bought a Lexus SUV, and I paid cash for it. I could afford to do this; by this time, I had saved close to a million dollars. Then a strange thing happened. Maybe the dumbest thing I would ever do in my life, but also the most relevant. I did it for a myriad of reasons, most which were inexplicable back then.

I gave all my money away.

★   ★   ★

On the opposite side of the earth, I discovered thirteen months of sunshine. That was the tourism motto for Ethiopia, which does actually have a calendar of thirteen months. In this amazingly diverse place, I became enlightened by the people and the culture. The glint of change sparked inside of me.

I want something more.

Strolling through Addis Ababa, the largest city in Ethiopia, I soaked in a feeling of contentment. I had come here with some friends to help build houses and ended up falling in love with the place. Early in the morning, the sun burst bright and the people were abuzz outside. They weren't over-westernized as in so many other foreign cities. The people in Addis Ababa loved me and my nature, my spirit. Every day I trained and later I meditated in the temples. People would ask for your help, so I'd hand out a couple of bucks to these people, knowing the American dollar went much further here. I had seen a lot of homeless people in my life, but homelessness in Ethiopia was of an entirely different kind.

One day I came across a man who didn't have legs and only had one arm, and instinctively I reached in my pocket to grab some bills. This day, however, I didn't have any cash on me, and neither did the guys I was with. The man on the side of the road smiled up at me, speaking in his native language, which I didn't understand.

"What'd he say?" I asked my friends. "Can you tell him I'm sorry, that I don't have any money?"

"He's blessing you," one of the guys said. "He says he can see that you have a big heart."

I stood there in disbelief. Here was this homeless man giving me a blessing and a beaming smile. It was the biggest smile I'd ever seen coming from someone who didn't have anything. My eyes welled up as I realized a truth.

We're so selfish, I thought. *We're so ungrateful for our lives. Americans are so content, so complacent. This guy right here has absolutely nothing but he carries the most positive attitude.*

I wanted that kind of attitude and that sort of heart. Later on I went back to that same spot to try to find the man, but I never did.

This was when I realized I wanted something bigger, something better than what I was doing. I wanted to help others. Giving someone on the street some money was one thing, but what I longed to do was offer hope to the hopeless. To share my heart with those with broken hearts. On that first trip of many to Africa, I decided I wanted to help people in a very real way.

I knew I didn't need a church to take a mission trip. I didn't need an organization to sponsor a child. And I didn't need an offering plate to give money to the poor. Sometimes you just go and find the needy and then figure out how to help them out. That's what I wanted to do.

After hiring a lawyer, I spent twelve months figuring out a plan to help bring some people from Africa to the United States. Back then, the only way for refugees or people from another country to come to America was by lottery, and chances were few. I had a friend who helped her brother do this. Her brother was eighteen when they first started the process, and when they finally got him to the United States, he was twenty-eight years old. And that was only one person. Now it's a little bit different, but back then it was virtually impossible to bring someone to the States in the regular, legal way. So I decided to speed up the process in my own way. Of course, nothing in this world is free, especially for people who don't have a lot.

When I went back to Africa, I brought two other people with me. We had to bring in a lot of money to help bring back some refugees. As a matter of fact, we ended up bringing $50,000 in cash. The reason we were bringing all that money was because I knew that we needed enough not only to help bring people back but also to pay for all their needs. We were helping to build a house and to assist people in desperate need too. This was the first time I'd ever physically seen that much money, and at first we had no idea how to carry all this money with us. The US charged you for every ten grand you had, so we needed to conceal it. A gym bag or several briefcases weren't going to do it, so we had to be creative.

People don't understand this about a lot of other cultures, whether they are African or Mexican or whatever. These people work their asses off, working five jobs at a time, saving money, having a dozen or more people living in a house with everybody working and saving money. They save to help their families, and having someone be able to come to America is a dream come true. The land of plenty, the land of opportunity, the American dream.

When me and these two ladies were about to board the plane carrying the hidden cash, I looked at them and saw their expressions. They looked so guilty! "Would you just relax?" I said to them. "This is going to work."

This was back in the late 1990s, when people took pictures with cameras, not phones. And they actually went out and developed the photos and put them in albums. So in each of our backpacks, we had these photo albums, the sort where you slid the photo into a clear plastic sleeve. There were four slots per page and all of them were filled with photographs.

When we went through security, an agent told us to stop to check our bags. I knew this was going to happen; it was inevitable. They laid out our bags on a table and then asked us how much money we had. One of the girls said she had $7,000.

"Seven thousand dollars?" the agent asked, skepticism in her voice. She looked at the girl and grinned. "If you got seven thousand dollars, I know you got more."

My friend should have said she had much less, but she chose to go with a strange half-truth, making it look suspicious. A second woman came and they began to go through our backpacks, taking out the photo albums and leafing through the pages. There were multiple books with full pages consisting of wedding photos, baby pictures, family shots, everything. Security asked why so many. As the agents looked through our items, they asked why we were going to Africa and where we worked. I revealed where I worked and the woman didn't believe me.

"You don't work at the Pentagon and the White House!" she said as she laughed at me.

"I do," I said.

She couldn't believe it, so she asked me if I knew a friend of hers who worked at the White House.

"Of course I know him," I said about the Secret Service agent. "That's my guy."

"Are you serious?" she said, still not believing me.

I grinned. For some reason, I had my badge on me, so I showed it to her. It had my ID and credentials with it. The woman now beamed with excitement, her entire attitude changing.

"No, no—no need for that," the woman told the other agent, who was still going through the photo albums. "They're good. Let them go."

So the girls grabbed their bags and scurried up to the plane. Security thankfully didn't find the crisp hundred-dollar bills we had carefully ironed, folded in half, and stuck behind each photograph. Every single photo had a bill hidden behind it. As the girls sat in their seats on the airplane, they were both saying, "Thank you, God! Thank you, God!" I looked at them and laughed.

"Thank God? No, you need to thank me! That was all me. Thank my credentials!"

Of course, I was joking. I thanked God the most for getting us out of that situation.

★ ★ ★

This was one example of my attitude at this time. I was young and irresponsible, but not in the way most young people were. I found ways to help as many people as I could. Family members, friends, kids, programs, anything that I could benefit. I wasn't being strategic with my giving and it wasn't something planned out. I wasn't doing it for any reason other than it felt right at the time. When somebody struck me as needing a leg up, I decided to help out, and I ended up exhausting all my money.

I needed to know the answer to a couple of questions for myself.

If I give all this money away, will I ever be able to earn it back? Was all of this pure luck, or did I really accomplish something on my own?

So I decided to keep $2,000 for myself and give everything else away. Of course, there was a moment when, after the dust settled and I only had two grand, I asked myself what I had just done. But I realized quickly that this forced me to start over again. It made me do a reset. This reset my mind, it reset my thoughts, and it reset my passion. It reset my drive, my resiliency. It was a complete and total personal overhaul. With that $2,000 that I had, I began again. I continued my journey in life with nothing but the $2,000 I set aside for myself.

I never made that million dollars back because I didn't try as hard. I made enough money back to keep doing what I needed to do, and then I refocused. During all this time, I was attending school, picking up degrees and habits and, most importantly, knowledge. I was picking up all this wisdom, and that was the best money I've ever earned. Mind you, I've had a couple hundred thousand dollars stolen from me. I've had business partners who robbed me and deals that have gone wrong. I don't get mad about the money being gone; my anger comes from knowing how I could have helped others with that money that is now gone.

Maybe I was crazy for giving all my money away, and if I am, maybe I should blame my mother. She's the one who gave me this big, beating heart of mine. She's the one who would invite people off the street into our home for a warm meal. I will never forget what she told me and my sister the first time this happened, the first time she welcomed someone into our home.

"You help as many people as you possibly can because they're people," my mother explained. "Some people are not as fortunate as us."

★ ★ ★

There was an unfortunate conclusion to the story about me setting up that bank account before going to Korea, but it was another important lesson I learned the hard way.

Years later, when I was at West Point in New York, I asked the family member who had been helping me with the account what the balance was, and they told me they didn't know. I immediately called the bank up to ask them about this account. It had been so long—twelve years—that they told me they couldn't give me the information. Honestly, I had forgotten that I was still putting money into this bank. This was where I was putting all my savings that were going to be there after I left the Army.

Eventually a woman at the bank was able to check on the balance.

"It looks like this account has a negative balance of one hundred dollars."

"I'm sorry?" I asked.

She told me again that it was negative one hundred dollars.

"What do you mean negative one hundred dollars? I'm talking about this account." I read off the account number again.

Once again they confirmed that it had a negative balance. They also informed me of something else, something just as bad. The $1,500 dollars that I had charged to help build up my credit should have been paid off *years* ago. But the family member who should have done this never did. Because of my age and my lack of any credit, they were charging me 30 percent interest including late fees on this, so I now had a balance of $18,000 dollars.

As the woman talked, she could sense me decompressing. She explained that this family member responsible for the account had not only taken all the money in it, but had also let the $1,500 go into credit. They would pay $20 on it to keep it active, then let it sit for months before paying another $20.

They kept it alive by spending money on it, drawing interest on it every time. This had gone on for twelve years.

This bank account was going to be my retirement money. I had been putting away $700 a month by this time, and that was a lot of money for me at the time. This account was the extent of what I was worth financially. Of course, this was my thinking at the time. I wasn't thinking big and I didn't have big numbers to work with, but then, that was where I was coming from. When I asked the woman at the bank to show me how much I had deposited into the account over the years, she said she would send the number to me. When I finally received it, the information stated that I would have had around $100,000 in my bank account if this relative hadn't been taking it.

Right away I did the only thing I could think to do: call my mother. I explained to her what happened, but instead of encouraging me or giving me advice on what to do, she gave another response.

"Go pray on it."

Go pray on it? That's not what I wanted to hear! Naturally I got upset. Mom was telling me that this was okay, that maybe my relative needed this.

"Mom—do you understand how much money this is?" I said.

I know she didn't, but even if she did, it didn't matter to her. She would have given me the same answer with any amount. That just showed my mother's generosity. Of course, I was furious, telling my mother what happened was wrong. I didn't talk to this person for over a year. I did what I always do; I disassociate. I move on. But now my mother wanted me to stop and pray on it!

"If I pray on it, are they going to give me my money back?" I said half-jokingly to my mom.

Here's the truth of the matter: I couldn't pray on it. Not at first. I had saved up my entire life to not be in a situation like this, and suddenly a family member had put me in this place. I was hurt and emotional. But as my mom always said, emotions can make you do things that you can't take back.

Eventually I did pray on it. We were a religious family and I grew up in the church, and despite all the things I'd seen while being in the military and in the world, I still could pray about this. I never did receive an apology from the person who did this, but I did receive a card that simply said, "I love you. Thank you for being you." I tore up that card and threw it away, but then I forgave this person. Maybe they were in a bad place, and maybe they had no other choice. A hundred different maybes went through my mind, just like they always did. To this day, we're still friends, and we still love each other. Every time I ever came home, I still gave this person money, even when they didn't ask.

This was a hard lesson that I learned, but it taught me a lot of things. As I always say, my mother fucked me up with my heart and giving. I've spent so much more money than I've earned. The world is full of takers, but they won't change how much I give.

It's one thing to have wealth, but it's a whole other thing to have relevance and a voice in today's culture. The vampires out there who want to suck you and your energy and your soul won't be able to do that if you continue to be true to yourself and your character. If you do something for money, then it will matter when that money is taken from you. But no troll can steal your character, and no thief can steal your compassion.

It's one thing to pray for someone who has taken something from you, but a whole other thing to keep giving to them. But I know now that this was part of my therapy, part of my letting go of the pain of the past. I also know that if God had not taken care of me after losing all this money, I would have been in the worst possible place. But I got back what was taken from me tenfold. No . . . a hundredfold.

It doesn't matter who you are and how much you're worth and what circumstances you're in. You can choose to be a beggar or a blessing.

THE DAY THE WORLD
CHANGED—9/11

The attack took place on American soil, but it was an attack
on the heart and soul of the civilized world. And the world
has come together to fight a new and different war, the
first, and we hope the only one, of the twenty-first century.
A war against all those who seek to export terror, and a war
against those governments that support or shelter them.

PRESIDENT GEORGE W. BUSH, 10/11/01

remember this day every day.

I remember the smell.

I remember the cries.

I remember when the world watched as America got struck
down, and I remember when the entire world decided to come
together and stand as one.

This day is a big reason why I do what I do.

Sometimes I don't want to remember this day, but I know I
need to remember.

God, I wish 9/11 had never happened.

★ ★ ★

The morning is beautiful. The sun starts to shine before 7:00 a.m. across a clear sky that begins to turn blue. I arrive at the Pentagon early as usual. I do everything around here, from cooking and planning menus to preparing for big and small events and exercising protocol. I've been here for five years, working for the chairman of the Joint Chiefs of Staff, having done things with General Powell, General Shalikashvili, and most recently General Shelton. Around 24,000 people work here in our country's military command center.

I'm strolling down one of the halls in this massive concrete structure. Over six and a half million square feet of space. The largest office building in the world. They broke ground on the five-sided building on September 11, 1941. Sixty years later, the Pentagon remains impressive and daunting. If you've ever been inside it, you will know it's like a community. There is a center court corridor with trees and birds, and each side of the building has a different story to tell.

We all have to wear badges, and sometimes I end up getting harassed about mine. It doesn't matter where I might be. I can be sitting down during a break and someone will walk by, spot me, and then ask, "Where's your badge?" I'll answer by saying, "What? This badge?" They tell me it needs to be visible, and every time I can't believe it.

Okay, fuck. Here we go again. There are a million people in here, but you see this big black kid right here and you gotta ask about his badge.

My badge is Pentagon Federal, the kind that only gets you into the offices and nowhere else.

Donald Rumsfeld serves as the secretary of defense, having started in January 2001 to work under President George W.

Bush. This is his second time as secretary of defense, first serving under President Gerald Ford from 1975 to 1977. I will see Rumsfeld down at the PAC (Pentagon Athletic Center), where we both work out. Whenever I walk by him, he smiles and says, "You're a big guy." I see Rumsfeld playing racquetball all the time; he is a great racquetball player.

These guys I train from the Department of Defense Pentagon tell me about Rumsfeld. I love training the DOD squad because we train so hard and because I always whup their asses in the process. They joke and tell me how Rumsfeld never lets them get near him for security. "Don't come near me!" Rumsfeld orders them. "I don't need security." They end up being a hundred meters away from him, and they tell me that it doesn't matter who he is, that they need to be close to him because this is the Pentagon. Anything could happen. They eventually wear him out and are able to get close to him to do their jobs.

At the same time I'm greeting familiar faces in the hallway on this Tuesday morning, five men with ties to al-Qaeda pass through security at Dulles International Airport and board American Airlines Flight 77. Right as I'm preparing for another busy day at the Pentagon, the airplane takes off at 8:20 a.m. bound for Los Angeles, California. Just over an hour later, all sixty-four people on board Flight 77 will be dead.

★   ★   ★

There is before and after. There is the person I was before that first plane hit the World Trade Center and the person I became when the dust and ashes settled. I will sometimes use this expression when I speak about 9/11: It was the first time I realized that this was an experience I would never forget.

None of us will.

I don't talk about this a lot because it's not my platform. I don't want anybody to feel sorry for me. I've never wanted anybody to know what happened to me on this day and afterward, until now. This is the first and only place where I will share all of this openly.

★   ★   ★

I'm watching the news on television with a group of people. A plane has hit one of the Twin Towers of the World Trade Center in New York. Somebody tells me about it and says it looks like an accident. An announcer says that witnesses describe it as a small commuter plane crashing into the building. As helicopter footage shows the dark smoke spewing out of the sides of the tower, there's an explosion.

"Another plane just flew into the second tower," a stunned Jon Scott on the Fox morning news show says. "This raises—this has to be deliberate, folks."

There is no question: America is under attack.

As we come to learn, that first plane wasn't a small commuter plane but a hijacked Boeing 767. American Airlines Flight 11 is carrying ninety-two people when it crashes into the North Tower at 8:46 a.m. The second plane is also a 767 that's been taken over by terrorists. United Flight 175 explodes into the South Tower at 9:03 a.m. and all sixty-five aboard perish.

It's impossible to know how many fatalities these two crashes will cause.

Thirty-four minutes after that second plane strikes the South Tower, there is a blast that hits the Pentagon with a force so hard and so thunderous that the entire building shakes. That's when I realize the attack has come to our front door. No . . . it's blown right through the doors and impaled our heart.

★ ★ ★

Everything moves in slow motion.

Everything is intensified.

Everything seems to be ringing with alarm.

Every sensation is heightened. Everything you see and smell and hear and taste.

Everything feels surreal, but you know this is really happening. And you know you have to spring into action.

★ ★ ★

As alarms and sirens are going off in the background and people are yelling to evacuate, we rush outside without knowing what happened. I have no idea what just took place. Men and women are crying and yelling and screaming. There is a lot of confusion. People don't understand what's going on until they exit the Pentagon, out onto the center court, and see the smoke and then realize, *Oh my God, we're under attack.* This is a terrorist attack. The Twin Towers were attacked and now the Pentagon's been attacked.

This realization, this horror, doesn't stop me from moving. One thing I know that I do whenever there is danger is to reach out to others to help them. That might mean I forget to help myself. It's kind of like when the oxygen masks pop out on a plane, you're supposed to put one over your mouth before helping anybody else. This is never a thought that comes to mind, however.

There's one guy who was closer to the blast, and I fall in with him and a couple other guys to go back in and see what we can do to help.

★　★　★

There are things that I want to tell that I won't. Things that I've seen. Things I remember.

Then there are the things I want to see and remember but I can't.

I remember as much as I can, but there are holes in my memory that are black and empty.

Pieces of that day float away like ashes. Others remain buried deep inside, portions that I cannot talk about. That I shouldn't unearth.

★　★　★

"This is a tragic day for our country. Our hearts and prayers go to the injured, their families and friends."

I watch as Donald Rumsfeld speaks to the world at a news briefing about the Pentagon attack on the evening of 9/11. Also in attendance is the chairman of the Joint Chiefs of Staff, General Hugh Shelton, Thomas E. White, the secretary of the Army, and Senators Carl Levin and John Warner.

"We have taken a series of measures to prevent further attacks and to determine who is responsible," Rumsfeld says. "We're making every effort to take care of the injured and the casualties in the building. I'm deeply grateful for the many volunteers from the defense establishment and from the excellent units from all throughout this region. They have our deep appreciation."

I think back to earlier that day when there were thousands of people standing and watching and waiting to know what was happening. All the confusion—just hours and hours of confusion. Rumsfeld speaks as he always does, with authority and certainty.

"It's an indication that the United States government is functioning in the face of this terrible act against our country. I should add that the briefing here is taking place in the Pentagon. The Pentagon's functioning. It will be in business tomorrow."

It will be in business tomorrow.

The sentence strikes me when I first hear it. I'm surprised to hear that everybody will be back at work tomorrow. A few moments later, Rumsfeld takes some questions from reporters. One goes back to this statement he made.

"Mr. Secretary, you said that the Pentagon would be open for business tomorrow. What kind of assurances can you give the people who work here at the building that the building will be safe?"

"A terrorist can attack at any time at any place using any technique. It is physically impossible to defend at every time in every place against every technique. It is not possible to give guarantees. The people who work in this building do so voluntarily. They're brave people, and they do their jobs well."

So we're showing them we're still brave and we're not defeated by going back to work?

Our secretary of defense's attitude is that we can't let the enemy think they've won. That might sound good on paper, but the reality on the ground is that people have died in their own backyard, and their friends and coworkers need time to grieve and get themselves right. It shocks me that they expect all of us to soldier on after such horrific acts. But this pretty much seems to be the message we get.

Do your job, don't talk about it.

That's no problem because that's what I've done my entire life.

★ ★ ★

So many lives are lost. People are hurting and spirits have been broken, but other spirits have become intertwined and entangled and even reinforced. Everything changes after that day. Everyone talks but all I hear is whispering and weeping. All I see are tears on other faces and on my own. Tears and a little hate. I know they say you shouldn't hate, but "hate" is the word I use for the people who took so many lives and changed so many things for no reason. I am ready to go to war just like everybody else, but for the time being, I can only do one thing. So I volunteer my services to be part of the recovery after the brutal attacks on 9/11. And recovery is exactly what it sounds like. You recover things. In this case, we're searching for "anything" that could be used to identify those who perished, for their family members.

In the definitive account of the Pentagon attack, titled *Pentagon 9/11*, the Department of Defense Historical Office details everything that took place that day. It is easier to quote two passages about recovery teams rather than trying to sum up my own experience.

The dead remained. Some were entombed under tons of rubble, some perished intact in their offices, some lay in stairwells or corridors where they had tried to escape, and some bodies were too battered or fragmented to be identifiable. Remains recovery proceeded in two steps— locating and removing bodies from the building, and sifting through debris gathered and deposited in North Parking. The difficult task of searching the wreckage for victims or parts of them, documenting their whereabouts, and removing them for identification fell principally to Federal Emergency Management Agency search and rescue teams, Army engineers, FBI agents, Marine Corps photographers, cadaver dogs and their handlers, and the young soldiers of the Old Guard (3rd Infantry Regiment) from Fort Myer. Not until 26 September was this sad work declared finished.

The recovery process itself is a nightmare out of a horror movie.

Searchers often had to make their way through several feet of rubble. Water from broken mains and fire hoses had pooled on the floors six inches deep and even knee-high in some areas. Ceiling grids sagged, electrical wiring snaked down walls and across floors, and plastic light fixtures melted by intense fire hung down like ribbons of caramelized sugar. Plumbing, burned batteries, twisted pipes, heating ducts, and air conditioners were heaped among the ruins, along with jagged metal, nails, and broken glass. Wood, plaster, and tiles had fallen from the floors above. Desks and filing cabinets were reduced to scrap metal. Asbestos lay exposed and lead paint peeled off walls. A layer of black soot covered virtually every surface. Without lights it was pitch dark; even with flashlights dust in the air limited visibility to ten feet in places. The noxious atmosphere and standing water carried the threat of infectious disease. Fires still smoldered, adding to the acrid stench and smell of decay from the jet fuel, burned plastic, metal, and human flesh.

This is the scene I see, the picture seared onto my soul. I end up being part of the recovery, but neither I nor the military wind up participating in my own recovery from the horrors I experienced.

★   ★   ★

The plane crashing into the Pentagon ends up killing 125 people inside. The oldest is seventy-one, while the youngest is three. Altogether, the 9/11 attacks result in 2,977 perishing and more than 6,000 others injured.

There is crying, there is anger, there is sadness, there is hugging, there is a lot of confusion. Some people don't realize how devastating the Pentagon attack really was until later. Some people don't understand the impact and the severity of the destruction.

No one knows how it will shape the rest of our lives.

Soon after the attacks come the conspiracy theories. There are so many. The one that I hear often states that a rocket struck the Pentagon instead of an airplane. I can say with absolute authority that it was not a rocket but a plane. A very fast-moving plane. Since I was part of the recovery team, I know this with a haunting certainty.

Looking at the devastation, you realize what one country can do to another country and to so many innocent people when you have so much hate behind it. But you also can see the phoenix rising from the ashes, a country bonding together. For the first time in our history, there isn't any black or white. There aren't yellows, reds, or mixed colors. There is just red, white, and blue. There are countrymen and countrywomen. There are supporters, people who sign up by the thousands to join the military, folks who want to fight for our country. Everybody from celebrities to professional athletes to retired civilians wants to pitch in.

This is the day that the world changes. It's not just Washington, DC, or New York City that changes, and not just the United States.

THE DAY THE WORLD CHANGED—9/11 ★ 119

This is the day that every person in America and other countries around the world comes together for something greater.

★   ★   ★

"If there's anyone that may need to talk to someone about this, then you need to talk to someone."

This is what we are told by the military not long after the attacks. They announce that they're bringing in a team of mental health advisers in case anyone wants some counseling. This is one of the times when I hear the term "PTSD" mentioned. At the time I don't know what post-traumatic stress disorder even means.

As I talk to military and DOD officers and workers, I discover that many of them are going to these counselors because they're struggling with the aftermath of the attack, especially having seen the things the recovery teams saw. I decide that maybe it will be a good thing for me to go talk to someone too, so I go up my chain of command and ask to be put on the list. Since I have a special security clearance level, I need to get an approval from a supervisory team before connecting with a counselor.

When I go to them to talk about getting counseling, I hear a very different message than the one that's been coming from the military.

"Hey, Chef. Do you like your job?"

"Roger," I answer.

I understand exactly what they're saying. They're telling me I have to choose between keeping my job and getting counseling, that they don't have time for things like that, especially now, after 9/11. At this time, there is still an attitude among many military higher-ups that a soldier admitting that he or she needs help—or, God forbid, harbors thoughts of suicide—is a disgrace. At this moment, I know where things stand. So I walk away from the thought of asking for help.

The Pentagon attack on 9/11 leaves me with a constant cough and a life full of nebulizers and inhalers. A doctor tells me this is the result of being there in the Pentagon and inhaling the equivalent of a thousand cigarettes at once. But it's the deeper injury that is more deadly. It's a wound that won't be healed, a wound that will need to be attended to. But I won't begin to heal this wound until many years later.

For the time being, the way I cope is by throwing myself into my work. Cooking becomes my therapy.

A GHOST FELL
IN LOVE WITH ME

If you judge people, you have no time to love them.

MOTHER TERESA

"**K**eep your jacket on."

This was the one piece of advice I received from the sergeant major before I interviewed to be an aide to a high-ranking admiral who was taking over as the secretary of the Navy. He was stationed in the Navy Yard, so I traveled there in my Class A uniform to meet the admiral and his wife. This was a couple of years after 9/11. I could have been told what sort of questions to ask them or what the admiral's personality was like, but no—I was simply told to keep my jacket on.

"Your skills are immaculate," the master sergeant said over the phone. "They're amazing. But just keep your jacket on."

"Roger. I'll do that."

I knew the connotation behind his statement. I carried this with me on a daily basis.

I arrived at the Navy Yard, where the sergeant major escorted me to the admiral and his wife at their quarters. The admiral was impressed as he read my evaluation and history. Since it was a stifling day in DC, I couldn't help sweating, and I couldn't hide the fact either.

"Sergeant Rush," the admiral said. "You can take off your jacket."

"Sir, I'm fine," I replied. "It's really no big deal."

"No, please. Go ahead."

"I'm comfortable with it, sir," I said, knowing how difficult it was to get the jacket off.

The admiral wasn't taking no for an answer. "I insist."

Fuck.

I unbuttoned my Class As and thought of the sergeant major's advice. I took pride not only in my work habits but also in my physique and how I took care of myself. Back then I was bigger than I am now, so as I tried to slip my jacket off, it got stuck on my arms, making me work and sweat even more. When I finally took it off, my arms were a lot more noticeable in my short-sleeved white shirt.

"Oh, my," the admiral's wife said in surprise as she looked at me.

Fuck, I kept thinking.

"I think I may be a little intimidated by you," she said.

Suddenly I found myself picturing this scene as if it were a cartoon. Here's the little white woman sitting next to her husband, who is a little white man who also happens to be an admiral in the Navy. They're interviewing this big black guy to come work for them. I can't help thinking of the irony of her statement.

Why are you intimidated by me? You should be motivated by me, because I'm going to be the person who protects you the most.

When she said that, I knew I was done with this interview, that their minds had already been made up. Or at least her mind, which meant both of their minds. The next thing she said only confirmed what I was thinking.

"The last aide we had listened to rap music. Do you listen to rap music?"

Seriously? I knew their last aide was a black guy.

"No, ma'am, I don't, actually. And if I did, it wouldn't be in a work situation."

Her next few comments had more racial undertones, so as she continued to talk, I began hearing Charlie Brown's teacher speaking from *Peanuts:* "Wah wah, wah wah wah wah. Wah wah wah? Wah wah wah wah."

This was my way of combating this situation, of realizing I was being judged based on my appearance instead of my abilities. As I was leaving, the sergeant major who was in charge walked me out.

"I'll let you know how you did," he told me.

I already knew how this had gone, so he didn't need to inform me, but shortly after the interview, the sergeant major called me.

"I hate to tell you this, but you're overqualified," he said.

I laughed at him. "Overqualified, huh? Okay, thanks for telling me that."

The irony of this came years later when this same sergeant major was working for a four-star general who was also black and an athletic freak. This general said he wanted Chef Rush, that I was the epitome of what he stood for. He wanted somebody standing beside him with a big, impressive physique who also embodied professionalism. When the former sergeant major called me with this great opportunity to work for the general, I listened to the offer to meet with him.

"I'm sorry," I said without any pause or reservation. "I think I'm overqualified."

It felt good to say that years after the incident with the admiral and his wife.

The truth is that some people can't see beyond the presence in front of them, so they never know the level of performance a person can bring. Fortunately the job with the admiral and his wife didn't work out. If it had, then I never would have met the Hagenbecks, who would change my life in so many ways.

★ ★ ★

One thing a lot of people don't know about generals is how vital their wives are to their success. The generals who listen to their wives are rewarded, while the ones who refuse to listen usually are not. The wife controls everything going on in their household and is crucial to making their lives run smoothly.

In 2006, I was requested for another interview to be the senior enlisted aide to Lieutenant General Franklin Hagenbeck, who was going to be the next superintendent at West Point. The general had commanded at every level in the Army and served four tours in the Pentagon on the Army and Joint Staffs. In the fall of 2001, he led the first forces into Afghanistan, and he was the senior commander there during the first defeat of the Taliban. His many awards and decorations included two Distinguished Service Medals.

Sometimes I interviewed with a general and his wife, but in this case, I only met with Judy Hagenbeck. By this time, I was a little deflated, since a lot of people had the same sort of reaction to me that the admiral's wife had. Maybe I was too black for them or too big for them—I didn't know and didn't care. I just knew I had all these skills and talents that I brought to the table. When I sat down with Judy, I had no clue what to expect.

Right away I discovered that Judy Hagenbeck was a very proper and very sweet lady. Everything about her exuded excellence. As we discussed the position, she asked me the sort of questions one might be asked in a job interview. We smiled and laughed and talked. It didn't feel like a formal interview but rather a casual conversation. I had no idea how it went, but I did leave being highly impressed by Judy and her husband.

Later on I found out that right after the interview, Judy had picked up the phone and told the general's aide-de-camp and chief of staff how much she loved me and wanted me to work for them. She had already interviewed all these senior guys who tried out for this job, one of the most prestigious jobs in the Army. They had experience and I was still raw. Judy put her faith in me and bypassed the rest, and that was truly unbelievable.

I ended up going to West Point in advance of Lieutenant General Hagenbeck arriving so I could shadow the general who was there, Lieutenant General Lennox. I was able to work with him and his guys to get an understanding of how things worked. The United States Military Academy is very different from other military installations, so I learned a lot in a short period of time.

When General Hagenbeck, known to everybody as Buster, and Judy arrived at West Point, I poured myself into my role as their senior aide. My entire job depended on excellence, and since I'm a Virgo, everything I did went into making this whole experience come to life for them. I was meticulous with everything, meaning I not only made sure to dot the i's and cross the t's but dotted and crossed them two times and three times and ten times.

Judy basically took me under her wing, telling me things and showing me things, not only giving me the insights of an officer's wife but also offering a different mindset to an enlisted soldier like myself. A mindset I would never have gotten the opportunity to see otherwise. We discussed everything. Sometimes I'd work eleven or twelve hours a day by my own choice, since I was a sponge soaking in everything I could possibly learn, but also because I enjoyed the Hagenbecks' company and conversation. I felt like these two people truly respected me and deserved my full attention, so I gave them everything I could.

Judy and Lieutenant General Hagenbeck always wanted me to be with them.

Every time I prepared a meal that was spectacular, they brought me and my team out to compliment us. They always introduced me, calling me by my rank and bragging about me.

In a place ruled by officers or seniors, the Hagenbecks gave a black enlisted soldier the opportunity to be their senior aide, and to have authority over so many things, from signing for their priceless quarters to handling different accounts for them. And I was given so much freedom to do things the way I wanted them done. They trusted me to accompany the lieutenant general to Iraq to be on his detail, trusting me to do the right things, even sometimes with their lives.

The Hagenbecks not only respected me by handing over this level of responsibility but also made me a part of their family. Yet even with them doing so, I never crossed the line. I always remembered that I worked for them. These were my principles. Over the years I opened up and even cried in front of Judy, only to have her hug me and tell me it was okay. At the time she was the only person I had to cry to. They always let me know that I was worthy all of the respect they gave me. I will always be appreciative of that.

★ ★ ★

"Sergeant 1st Class Andre Rush is a renaissance man of sorts."

I could never have imagined as a kid reading that opening line to an article in *Pointer View*, a publication for the US Military Academy at West Point. Especially since the article was all about me and my artistic abilities. Sure, maybe I could believe that something would be written about me serving in the military, but not about me drawing caricatures.

"Superintendent Lt. Gen. Buster Hagenbeck's senior enlisted aide has an imposing physical stature that rightfully places him as part of the Supe's security detail," the article says. "But in addition to that and managing the Supe's domestic affairs, Rush has other traits that add dimension to his character."

My artistic journey began when I was at the Pentagon working as the aide to General Hugh Shelton, who had retired. For the first time in seventeen years, since battery acid had destroyed my sketchbook, I decided to pick up a pen and put it to paper. I pressed the pause button to begin again, and I picked up right where I had stopped.

The idea came from my time with General Shelton and seeing all the special guests who signed his guest book, including presidents, kings, queens, prime ministers, coaches, celebrities, and other notables. Whenever I saw these people for the first time, I could picture what they would look like on paper, so I drew caricatures of them. My supervisor asked the protocol officer if I could do this for the guest book, but I was denied permission. Once again, someone above me didn't want my talents to shine. They didn't want me to get notoriety since the people signing the book, as well as the principal, would inquire about the artwork. I was still a small fish in the pond.

I decided to research the different kinds of products the publisher of our guest book produced. After discovering they made drawing paper, I asked if they could make a guest book with drawing paper on one side and the entry paper on the facing side. The publisher accommodated my request, so I had a custom-made guest book created for all the colorful visitors General Shelton entertained. The general and his wife loved it. All the guests assumed the illustrations were done out of house.

When I began working for Lieutenant General Hagenbeck after his arrival at West Point, I told him and Judy about the guest book. She welcomed it with open arms and shared that with *Pointer View*.

"I was thrilled when I saw the work he did prior to coming here," Judy said. "I knew he had a very artistic background, but I didn't know how much. This is just the tip of the iceberg on his talents."

For someone who has battled against so many not wanting me to succeed in my job, it was a breath of fresh air to work for the lieutenant general and his wife at West Point. Each time we had a special guest coming in, I drew a picture of them and something related to them. It might be a character trait, the college they went to, or a hobby they enjoyed. Since I stayed busy with many things at West Point, I rarely got the opportunity to meet the visitors before I drew them, so I researched them online to help get some facts on their lives. Many times I did these drawings minutes before the guest arrived. So while I would shop, prep, guide, direct, and prepare protocol and logistics, I used the minutes going back and forth to do my drawing.

I tried to use a couple different media to give some dimension to the painting, such as a charcoal pencil along with watercolor and acrylic paint. Next to people's pictures, I wrote their names and titles in calligraphy. When the guests came in, they signed their picture. Lieutenant General Hagenbeck loved to see what I created in the guest book, and the guests almost always commented on it.

I enjoyed drawing people; I could have fun. There were so many memorable people. I've drawn George W. Bush, Obama, Arnold, Coach K, and Tom Brokaw. I loved drawing the royalty, the sirs, the knights, the queen. They each brought a different vibe with them. And to be honest, if you asked me who and how many people I've drawn, I absolutely couldn't tell you. There have been so many.

This was an outlet for me, something I could do on my own and out of the spotlight and then take pleasure knowing the joy it brought. I've always loved making people happy and seeing them smile. It's one of the great pleasures and privileges of preparing food or promoting fitness. The caricatures were just another way to serve, especially knowing how much they meant to the Hagenbecks.

"He's very special to us," Judy was quoted saying about me. "We're very lucky to have him."

I was very lucky to have them too.

★   ★   ★

When I was working at West Point, I developed a reputation as something of a ladies' man. One lady in particular. Her name was Molly, and she was a young Irishwoman. She had worked for the first West Point superintendent, Sylvanus Thayer, and still had her quarters in the basement of the superintendent's house, known as Quarters 100. Molly was a mischievous gal who had a habit of making guests at the house feel a bit . . . unwelcome. Molly liked to let people know who was boss.

Molly was also dead.

Molly, you see, was the famous West Point ghost. During the years I worked there, she and I got to know each other well, and we formed a bond based on mutual respect.

Part of my job as enlisted aide to several superintendents was to oversee the historic residence where the superintendents traditionally lived. This was a building that had been the home of Sylvanus Thayer, the "Father of West Point," in the 1820s. The basement part of the house had been left essentially as it was in its original years. It was a historically preserved site, climate controlled, and partially supervised by a museum curator. One of my responsibilities was to keep a tight inventory of all the historic objects in the basement, and to coordinate events with the curator. Anything that happened related to the historic site, I was involved in it.

I'd heard about Molly my first day on the job. No one seemed to know too much about her, but she had a habit of messing with the personal belongings of overnight guests at Thayer House and "unmaking" their beds. Typical ghostly deeds like knocks on walls, cold spots, and weird noises were also attributed to her. Every once in a while, Molly would appear "in person" to someone too. Back in the early 1970s, William Knowlton, who was superintendent at that time, was so concerned about Molly that he asked Ed and Lorraine Warren to come to West Point. If you're any kind of horror fan, you know that the Warrens are that famous ghost-hunting couple who inspired *The Amityville Horror* and *The Conjuring*, among other movies. The Warrens conducted one of their classic paranormal investigations. Their conclusion? Thayer House was downright infested with ghostly activity.

I'll never forget my first "date" with Molly. I had both an upstairs and a downstairs office at the residence. The downstairs office was in an unfinished storage area outside the historic part of the basement. That part of the basement was dark and dingy but still had enough ambient light so you could see your way around. One day I went down there to get some paperwork. As soon as I stepped into the office, the door closed behind me. Okay, shit happens. I found the papers I was looking for, then turned around and opened the door.

Outside the doorway, there was total darkness. I mean blackness. No light whatsoever. And here's the really weird part: no light from inside the office was spilling out into the hall either. It was as if there was a wall of blackness outside that started at the door frame. It was the freakiest thing I'd ever seen. I was damn scared, but the man in me wasn't about to scream for help like a schoolkid.

I shut the door, paced around the office, picked up a few random objects, put them down again, paced around the room a few more times, and then went back to the office door and opened it again. Still a wall of darkness. Total silence too. My heart started jackhammering in my chest.

Calm down, Andre. There's a logical explanation here.

Like what? The sun just burned out? The whole house has been wrapped in a giant black trash bag? How could there be no light at all?

I took a few careful steps out into the pitch-black hallway, but it was impossible to see even six inches in front of my face. It was like being in a deep subterranean cave. And the silence was so complete, I could hear my own heart beating. I scurried back into the lighted office, shut the door again, and sat in the chair.

Okay, just breathe.

And then I did the only "logical" thing I could think of.

"Hi, Molly," I said, trying to speak in the most casual tone I could muster. "How are you? My name's Andre and it's a pleasure to meet you."

For the next ten minutes, I just sat there talking. I poured my heart out to Molly, sharing fears and secrets that I'd never told to a living soul. My instinct was that if I made myself open and vulnerable, Molly would see that I meant her no harm and that she could trust me. As I blabbed away like a crazy person, I got the strong sense that "someone" was listening.

When I had said all I could think to say, I stood up and said, "Thank you, Molly. I'm looking forward to seeing you again. I'm going now."

I walked to the door and opened it. This time there was light outside the door. Dim light, but the normal amount. Light beams from the office were once again passing through the door frame and hitting the floor in the hall. I could hear birds chirping and the distant sounds of cars and voices.

I'd like to say I felt total peace in that moment, but the truth is, I ran like hell. I tore up those stairs as fast as my feet could carry my 285-pound ass. I found my junior aide and said, "Listen to me. I want you to go upstairs and get that small throw rug. Then I want you to go downstairs and put it across the threshold so the office door will never close again."

"Why would you want me to—"

"Just do it!"

The poor dude went flying out of the room like he was the one who'd seen a ghost. I didn't tell anyone about what happened that day for a long, long time.

Molly seemed to accept me from that point on, probably because I always talked to her respectfully and asked her permission before doing anything new in the basement. She even showed herself to me a few times, which was something she rarely did, and would let me introduce visitors and VIPs to her. I once had the honor of introducing her to Tom Brokaw, for example. Shortly after I gave him that tour, he made a big donation to West Point and mentioned me in one of his pieces. There was even interest on the part of the *Ghost Hunters* TV show in doing an episode about Molly and me, but West Point decided it wouldn't be the best thing for the academy's image.

I had a lot of funny Molly experiences over the years. I especially enjoyed watching new hires "meet" her for the first time. More than once, I saw grown-ass adults run out of that building and refuse to come back. But Molly always "behaved" herself around me and stopped her mischief whenever I asked her to.

I sometimes wondered if it was more than mutual respect that created our "bond." Over the years, I asked lots of people about her story. I was never able to get the definitive truth on Molly, but one story I heard was this. When Molly worked at the academy, she took a shine to a young black man who worked there, and I guess he shined right back at her. In those days, of course, a white Irish girl and a young black man couldn't get cozy with each other. And they didn't. They kept their interactions proper and their "flirtations" subtle. But somehow word got out and somehow Molly ended up hanging from a tree for witchcraft.

Sometimes I wonder if I reminded Molly of her would-be lover, if maybe I was kind of a stand-in for him. Then again, I don't even know if that old story is true. But I do know that Molly was. After all, I dated the gal for years.

★   ★   ★

I told the story of Molly whenever I did the tours for West Point. People don't realize that West Point is one of the most visited places in the country besides the White House. It's so beautiful and so historic, and each season brings its own unique element to it. When you're on the grounds, you get to see every color of every rainbow that you didn't even knew existed. It feels like old England.

I enjoyed talking to the cadets when I gave tours. All of them coming there have been told that they're the best of the best, and some behaved as if they knew it and wanted others to know it as well. There were some who were humble and others cocky. It was fun to meet all of them while I gave my tours. Everybody at West Point knew me.

I shared the story about Molly with everybody—from presidents to Tom Brokaw—and I always said the same line:

"Molly had a crush on me. And she showed me herself because she had jungle fever."

Everybody always laughed at the joke. I had maybe said it a thousand times. Then one day, the sergeant major came to me after one of my tours.

"Hey, we got a complaint from a cadet about you saying the thing about jungle fever."

"Huh?"

I couldn't believe it, but I did know which cadet he was talking about. It was one who had gotten upset about the guys making fun of him since he kept looking at my triceps. The sergeant major told me I needed to stop joking around like that. I couldn't believe it.

"So you're discrediting me?" I said. "A black man saying jungle fever as a joke to a cadet who just got here who's also a white guy? I'm the black guy, but *he's* offended?"

"Yeah, Chef."

"Got it," I said.

★ ★ ★

I loved working for the Hagenbecks and being part of the Hagenbeck circus. But I worked my ass off at Quarters 100. So hard that I lost myself. I did everything from inside the quarters to the outside. I helped with a renovation taking place, including a new design of the quarters and the kitchen. I was fortunate that the Hagenbecks gave me leeway to do what I wanted, everything from picking out color codes to supervising staff to overseeing the thousands of guests we had coming to the quarters. There were house tours and ghost tours and tailgate parties at Quarters 100. I was involved with every aspect of running the place, including being responsible for seven different financial accounts.

All of this responsibility and authority would become a problem when the Hagenbecks left and a new general came in, but that was a distant thought during this time.

I took so much pride in the things I did at West Point. Everybody knew me; to this day, cadets I knew back then still reach out to me. I'm humbled by the respect and the responsibilities I had there.

When the general decided to retire in 2010, I was sad to hear the news. Lieutenant General Hagenbeck and Judy taught me a lot. Every principal I've worked for has taught me something, good or bad. In honor of my time with them, I gave the Hagenbecks the guest book full of so many drawings I had done and so many autographs of those famous people.

One day after retiring, the general called me up to ask if I could meet with him over coffee. When we met, we talked about business and a job opportunity he was passing on to me. He was continuing to teach me things even when I wasn't working for him. The Hagenbecks were integral in helping me know and never forget my own worth.

To this day I keep in touch with the general and his wife. Every so often, Judy reminds me that she's still looking out for me, that they say hello and that they're proud of me. Just four days ago, Judy texted me with a simple message:

I hope you are well. Always thinking about you.

They always made me feel worthy, and I hope I did the same for them.

TOXIC LEADERSHIP, COWARDS, AND A** KISSERS

A true leader has the confidence to stand alone,
the courage to make tough decisions, and the
compassion to listen to the needs of others. He does
not set out to be a leader, but becomes one by the
equality of his actions and the integrity of his intent.

GENERAL DOUGLAS MACARTHUR

There is a massive disparity in the military between those with swollen pride and others with shattered psyches. Rank plays a part in this, but ultimately it comes down to the recesses of an individual heart.

Over the years I've seen a lot of people who deserved to move up through the ranks, but I've also seen others who grew arrogant after making those steps up. Sometimes they can change overnight. The leaders with the most toxic egos always precipitate their own demise by seeing themselves as something more than they are and ignoring the sound advice of others around them.

No matter how big you are, there is always someone who is bigger. And no matter how broken you may be, there is always someone who has been in your shoes, or worse.

★ ★ ★

"Hey, Chef. There's a young sergeant over here at the company who's on compassionate reassignment. They say he's a cook but he's just sitting there being a desk jockey. Do you want to get him to come over and work for you?"

Compassionate reassignment is invoked when some sort of medical or traumatic emergency requires that a soldier move to another duty station to be closer to his family or to a facility.

"Give me his number."

Sergeant Durden was a young black man between twenty-five and twenty-seven years old. When I called him, the E5 was young but energetic as hell, a perky guy who had been in the military for eight or nine years.

"I heard you're over there doing nothing," I said. "How do you like it?"

"I don't like it," he admitted over the phone.

"Okay. Here's the deal. I'm getting you to work for me, but before you say yes, which you will, I'll let you know that I am going to work the shit out of you. I'm going to show you things. I'm going to teach you. I'm going to make you learn. It is going to be the hardest you've ever worked, but it's also going to be the most rewarding job that you'll ever remember."

"Okay," he said in a doubtful tone. "But I don't think they'll let me leave."

"You're already gone," I told him as I hung up the phone.

After making a call, I called Sergeant Durden back.

"Okay, report tomorrow."

"Sir? Are you serious?"

"Yeah."

Working as a senior aide and adviser to the superintendent of West Point means you're inside a principal's private quarters, and for me that meant I ended up doing everything. I was the keeper of the key, overseeing project management and security. I did the daily strategic planning and worked with protocol for visits. I had to sign for the quarters and I had tens of millions of dollars' worth of inventory under my watch.

When I brought Sergeant Durden in, I could see he had never been that close to a general and to this sort of lifestyle. The first month he was there, I worked him like a dog, telling him, "You're gonna learn all this." I prided myself on being an open book, especially with the knowledge I had acquired, because everybody had their book closed and locked and sealed and tucked away when it came to me. I told myself, *I'll never do that to anyone. I'll give them everything they need to succeed.* The only thing that I asked them in return was to share everything that I gave them. Don't be a hoarder of secret knowledge. Don't feel like you have to be that selfish person. If you worry about somebody taking over, then you shouldn't even be there in the first place.

After working there for a month, Sergeant Durden asked if he could speak with me one day. We went outside where we could talk in private.

"Thank you, Chef," he said as he began to cry.

He couldn't help the tears spilling out of his eyes.

"This is what I needed, coming here and working with you," Sergeant Durden said. "It's been such a gratifying experience. I want to let you know how much I appreciate you."

The young man then commenced to tell me why he was there on compassionate reassignment. The story was worse than I had imagined. I listened to him be vulnerable and show emotions, and afterward I gave him a hug and told him it was okay.

"You good," I said. "I got you. I got you."

After that, Sergeant Durden was my soldier. I became a mentor and a friend to him. I made it clear to him not to get things twisted. He still worked for me, but I was going to make sure the sergeant was taken care of mentally, emotionally, and physically. That's what leaders are supposed to do. We are there to take up for all soldiers and military members who are in need and who are under duress. If ever there was a young man who fit this category, it was Sergeant Durden. Soon after he was assigned to me, he began to thrive.

Seeing a soul change through doing something they love is inspiring to me, especially when I'm helping to stir that love. As the months passed, Sergeant Durden worked hard and loved learning all these new things he had never done before. He became infatuated with making pastries after he saw me making them. "Oh my God, Chef. How do you do that?" he asked me. He was hungry to learn and I was eager to teach. He was so proud of the things he learned to do, and he began doing them for his kids and his wife. Sergeant Durden didn't just have passion for baking; he also had the power and know-how to perform in the kitchen.

★   ★   ★

It was hard to see General and Mrs. Hagenbeck leave West Point when the general retired in 2010. The new general coming in asked me to stay, and I reluctantly remained in my position. I had never met the principal, so I didn't know a thing about him. I had no clue how things were about to change.

My job consisted of both helping the Hagenbecks move out and then moving the new general in. Since we were in the process of renovating Quarters 100, this made the move even more taxing than usual. As we were moving all of the new couple's stuff into the sixteen thousand square feet of space, I couldn't fathom the amount of shit they were bringing with them. The general's wife was there overseeing everything. I remember opening up all these boxes—hundreds of them, one at time—and they were all packed meticulously with paper.

"I want you to take all the paper and flatten it out so we can recycle it," the general's wife told me.

What the fuck?! There were thousands of pieces of paper.

"I'm saving the military money," she added.

I had two people helping me, Sergeant Durden and another guy who worked for me. Later on I told Durden I wasn't about saving all this paper.

"This woman's crazy," I said. "This shit is already accounted for, so this isn't saving any damn money. I can't do this. This is a waste of my time."

It wasn't a good start, and things only grew worse.

With Sergeant Durden there on compassionate reassignment, that meant he was working for me and not for Quarters 100. He'd been there for six months, and both he and his wife had been going to therapy. I decided to do what leaders do and tell the new general about Durden's situation.

"Sir," I told my new boss, "the sergeant here—the young soldier who's twenty-six—he's here on compassionate reassignment. I'd like him to stay, because this is why he's here."

The general was a tall man, and he sat upright as he looked down at me. "Let me check with my wife about that."

What the fuck? I thought. *Why the fuck do you need to check with your wife about a soldier's situation?*

I simply said, "Roger. Okay, sir." Then I left.

From the moment I began to work for the new principal, I noticed that he was very strange. As he was moving in, the general and his wife were getting ready to see his son who was overseas, but at the last minute the general backed out for some reason and decided to stay in his new accommodations. He also decided to let a woman he had brought in to work for him stay at his quarters while she was waiting for her housing situation to be finalized. This just so happened to be when his wife and kids were gone. Everybody knows what sort of impression this makes. For a leader in his position, this was dumb as fuck. Why would you do that?

On that Friday, I went to the general and told him I wouldn't be there over the weekend. I told him of the only plans that were on the schedule, some people coming into the house to do maintenance on Saturday.

"That's fine," the general told me. "Have them come over."

As a reminder, I left a note to the general on the table telling him what time the workers were coming over. I didn't think anything more about it until Monday morning, when the other soldier working under me called me. Sergeant Durden wasn't around, since the general didn't want him there.

"Hey, Master Sergeant," my soldier said. "The general wants to talk to you."

When I went to see the general, he had my soldier right in front of him.

"I thought I told you that I didn't want anybody around here this weekend."

"Sir, we talked about this. I left you a note on your table."

The general was indignant. "I didn't see any note. When I tell you to do something, I want you to do it."

"Roger."

I left with my soldier, analyzing the situation. I clearly had told the general about the people coming Saturday, and he had clearly explained that he was fine with it. Not only that, but I knew I had left that note on the table. Getting my soldier to call me to speak to him said a lot, and so did the fact that I had to stand in front of my soldier while the general chewed me out. My new principal deliberately wanted to emasculate me.

"I don't know why he did that," my soldier said.

I looked at the table but didn't find any note, so I went into the garage and found the note balled up and tossed in the garbage. Like the smart-ass that I am, I took the note out, uncrumpled it, then placed it back on the table. I didn't give a fuck who he was. If you fuck up, you fuck up. I didn't know if he threw it away or if the woman in the house tossed it, but it didn't matter.

You knew those people were coming.

When the people who came that Saturday visited the house to get the rest of the stuff, I asked them how it went and if there were any issues with the general.

"Oh, no. He was really nice and very hospitable. He actually had us stay around and showed us some of his stuff."

"Interesting," I said.

Once again, I knew how this was all going to play out. I had been here before too many times. After such a wonderful experience in this place with the Hagenbecks, another unfortunate situation had arrived at Quarters 100. I knew it was a circumstance of control, dominance, whatever the fuck you want to call it. I was enlisted personnel while this guy was the highest of the high. But here's another fact:

I know me. I know me.

Sometimes the guys who achieve a certain rank and a certain stature in the military can become complacent or entitled. This is common among those who achieves success, whether it's power or financial or anything else. If you started with nothing and you end up with hundreds of thousands of dollars, the chances are you will be grateful. I still tell myself all the time regarding money to always remember where I am from and why I do what I do. That's the just fact of the matter. Some people think that they are better than others, whether they forgot where they came from or grew up feeling that way.

With the new general, I explained what I did in my job. As I've said, I did a lot. Actually, I did more than a lot. I controlled all the situations at Quarters 100, not because I'm a control freak, but because I knew how everything worked, so I knew the quickest and most effective way to get things done. It took me a long time to learn this. After discovering all the things I did, the general told his chief of staff that he didn't want me in charge of all these tasks.

"Sergeant Rush, the general wants me to handle these things. Can you give me the details on everything and how they work?"

The chief of staff was a colonel, so he had rank. There were about a hundred different things that I had a program and system for, which I had spent years meticulously working on details for, and now he wanted to take over all of them. It didn't matter about this man's rank.

"Absolutely not," I said. "Figure it out."

I'm not giving you fucking six-plus years of work so you can take over instead of standing up and telling the general I have the legal authority to oversee all of this.

This chief of staff was not allowed to have control of everything because legally it could be a conflict of interest.

So with the new principal coming in, I ended up getting new attire made. I wore polo shirts and paid a lot of money for them since they were custom-made. I wanted to look as sharp as possible for the new guy as we held the first roundtable meeting with the principal. We were there to talk about the calendar and the upcoming events I helped plan. Our football games were big deals at West Point. In this roundtable, there was the general and other officers at the table, including the chief of staff. My aide-de-camp, the command sergeant major, was also there. As I had done thousands of times before, I was writing down notes in my notebook as we talked about the daily and the weekly duties. Out of the blue, the general called out my name.

"Sergeant Rush."

"Roger."

"I get it. You got your little muscles and you want to show off and lead by intimidation. You think you're me."

The comment came out of nowhere and reeked of contempt. The first thing I did was look at the people around the table, and the first thing every one of them did was look down and ignore the situation.

Here I go again.

"Sir, I don't think I am you. I do not lead by intimidation. I have been here for a very long time. I make things happen. I'm a representation of you. I do everything in accordance to you, to make you look good."

I felt fucking stupid telling this man this while these colonels and majors all remained silent. While this master sergeant explained to this goddamn general about the irrelevancy of his ego. The general didn't want to hear anything I said.

"Yeah, yeah, yeah. Here's the deal. I want you to take off that shirt and never wear it again." The general proceeded to tell me what sort of uniform he wanted me to wear. I couldn't believe it.

"Sir. You know, all of this is new. I just paid for it. For you. I paid for new clothes. You knew I was doing this, so why didn't you tell me this earlier?"

"Just make sure it doesn't happen again," the general said, dismissing my question.

At this point, I was at the highest level I could be as an enlisted soldier. I had done the highest tasks you could possibly think of. I had worked for presidents and the chairman of the Joint Chiefs of Staff and the secretary of the Army. I had been at the Pentagon on 9/11 and had spent time in Iraq and Afghanistan. After everything I had done, this bastard was in here talking about how I needed to take off my fucking shirt so I didn't show my muscles, just because he thought I was leading by intimidation.

After the meeting, I went to the sergeant major and wanted someone to back me, but I got nothing.

"Yeah. You know—he doesn't like me either," the sergeant major said.

You sorry piece of shit. Nobody had the backbone to say a thing. The chief of staff, a colonel, came to me to explain.

"It looks like he just doesn't like you, Master Sergeant."

"Okay, I'm good with that," I said. "I don't like him either."

"No—don't say that you don't like him," he told me.

"You know what? I'm going to say this to you. I don't fucking like him. Don't tell me that he doesn't like me and then tell me I need to like him. That doesn't make any sense to me. That's not going to happen." I paused and took a breath. "I don't even care. As long as he doesn't mess with my NCOER, I'm fine."

I was referring to my Army Noncommissioned Officer Evaluation Report (NCOER), which was what enlisted personnel used to get promoted to the next rank. The NCOER evaluated a soldier based on their performance and potential. While officers were sometimes automatically promoted, noncommissioned officers weren't. We could go from E1 to E4 automatically, but anything from E5 to E9 involved being promoted, so it was imperative to get good marks on your evaluation and to receive good comments from your supervisor.

For the last eight years, my NCOER had been consistently rated at the top all across the board, and this had come from the highest of generals. I had been doing this for a long time, and I took pride in my work and my reputation. Being promoted was a big deal; there would usually be a ceremony accompanying someone who'd been promoted. With all the promotions I had been given over the years in the military, I had never had any such thing. I would simply go and pick up my rank and wear it the next day without any fanfare.

Sure enough, when my next NCOER came, the general scored me low. I was pissed off. I'd done this job diligently for many years. I asked to speak to him to talk about my report and about the low marks he gave me.

"I did that so you can show some growth in your career, so you can show your progression," the general said.

You lying piece of shit. I'm already at the top of my career and you know that.

"Sir, I've never had these marks," I explained. "The last time was when I was an E5, which was thirteen years ago."

The general didn't want to hear what I had to say, and he didn't change anything in the evaluation. I knew he was doing this deliberately, but I didn't know exactly why.

Either you're a racist, a prick, an asshole, or just intimidated by me and you want to show some authority.

None of those designations mattered as much as the main one: he was a general. He was at the top of the food chain and there was nothing I could do. My mother's words rang through my head:

"Emotions can save lives and emotions can take lives. Emotions can put you in jail and emotions can make you do things that you can't take back."

I knew I needed to control my emotions. At the same time, I knew the general was trying to fuck with my livelihood. I was disappointed to discover that after all the time I had spent in this job and at this place, with so much of my heart and soul being poured into this position, no one, and I mean no one, stood by my side. I decided to go to the aide-de-camp to tell him about the situation.

The aide-de-camp is an officer who works on the staff of a high-ranking commander. This particular aide-de-camp was a major, and at that point I considered him a good guy. He was young, but that's just the nature of the military. I went to his little office and stood in front of him with the door shut, explaining what was happening and how the general was messing with my evaluations. The aide-de-camp nodded his head but explained there was nothing he could do about it. He knew the lieutenant general was wrong but had to stand on his side, so I persisted.

"No, I can't do this," I told him, continuing to explain what was happening. "You don't understand. The general is doing this deliberately and he's trying to—"

"At ease, Sergeant!" the aide-de-camp yelled. "Get to attention!"

He barked out a slew of commands at me from behind his desk, yelling at me about how things were going to be and how I needed to act. I knew the door was closed, so when he finished, I began to talk very clearly and carefully.

"Let me tell you something," I said. "If you ever raise your fucking voice at me again, I'm going to reach over here and I'm going to beat the shit out of you. This door is closed and it will be your word against mine. But the one thing that is not going to happen is you're not going to treat me like I'm your fucking kid because you have no backbone."

The young major looked at me and realized I had broken out of being the submissive soldier to being a grown man who he had been yelling at.

"I understand this is your career and understand you have a family," I told him. "I get that. And I don't give a fuck if you want to suck his dick and kiss his ass, but you're not going to do this to me. You can tell me there's nothing you can do, but to switch this around and say I'm wrong—that makes you a coward as a commissioned officer and a leader. That right there is the most despicable and toxic kind of leadership the Army doesn't need. You know what's happening is wrong, but you'd rather stand by than do what's right."

I understood that this was the military, that these were the protocols we had to abide by. I got that. But I also got that this was my livelihood they were fucking with. I knew I needed to control my emotions, and I knew deep down that I had PTSD. But I'd been dealing with this shit forever.

"I'm going to get the fuck out of your office before something more happens," I told him.

I left the aide-de-camp's office without any ass being whupped. The general refused to change my NCOER. The irony was that when my next evaluation came, I got promoted again. And like always, there was no celebration, no fanfare. In fact, the leadership around me didn't even know I had been promoted. It didn't matter. I continued to do my job, and nobody was going to stop me from doing the best I could.

★　★　★

I was still working with Sergeant Durden, the young, talented black soldier. The general wouldn't let him come over unless he needed help. The sergeant became infatuated with cooking, so I came up with a plan.

"You want to get out of the military?" I asked him.

"I want to get out," Sergeant Durden said. "I want to start my own bakery one day."

"So let's set you up for success. We're going to do this TV show, and I'm going to show you everything you need for it. You're going to do great things."

There was a popular reality television show called *Next Great Baker* that was coming out with its second season. The plan was for him to get on the show. I explained to Durden that that's all he needed to do.

"Listen, you're not going to win, but you don't need to. You don't need to because you are going to be that person people remember. You're going to be relevant. You're going to be that guy who was on the show that people talk about."

Sergeant Durden wasn't so sure at first. "What am I supposed to do? I just started baking."

"Do your best," I told him. "That's all you have to do. It doesn't matter if you don't win. Just don't be the first one kicked off."

Sure enough, when the show aired, there he was with his bright smile, introducing himself in his parade dress uniform. "I'm Sergeant Durden from Fayetteville, North Carolina." While he was there, we kept in touch by either talking on the phone or texting. I would always encourage him, telling him how proud I was of him and urging him to stick to the plan. I had told him the things he needed to do to get on the show.

"You're not going to win the show, but that's not why I'm telling you to go on there," I said to Sergeant Durden. "It's not always about winning. It's about being there. It's about the battle of getting on it. There are going to be a lot of people there. You've had five months of inconsistent training with me teaching you how to bake. These other men and women have had five years or ten years or fifteen years of consistent training. But you're in the military and you're harder than them. You're going to prove you deserve to be there."

Sure enough, in the first week, Sergeant Durden not only showed he deserved to be there but he also showed he could win the whole competition. He had one of the best cakes for the challenge, giving him a high ranking. He lasted several more weeks. One of the challenges was that they had to see who could stay the longest in a freezer. I had thought that was perfect for him, and sure enough, he killed it because this had nothing to do with baking and everything to do with those life lessons learned as you adapted in the military. He was likable, so I knew he would make it several shows. It was incredible for a guy who had the least amount of experience but the most resilience.

★ ★ ★

As this was happening, I was on my own reality show called *Who the F@@k Do I Work For?* The general had taken away all my responsibilities and had me working for his wife like a fucking little servant. She had me cooking for her and their friends. We would do meals for people, and even though they weren't supposed to happen and I knew that, I made a choice to go ahead and do them. I smiled the entire time I was there. I'm sure so many of these people thought I was an idiot simply because I acted like a submissive servant.

For one event for around fifty people, my other sergeant and I worked the meal. We worked our asses off and after everything was over, the general's wife came over and gave me a card. Now, I knew that anything like this was off the books and would be paid in cash, and many people assumed since you were in the military, your value was only seven dollars or so an hour. That's why I hated doing things with certain people.

When I opened up the card, all I could do was laugh. It was a Starbucks gift card for twenty dollars. Not only that, but it had a Christmas symbol on it, meaning it was from last Christmas and it was being recycled. That was my redemption for doing this party: a twenty-dollar fucking regifted Starbucks card.

The situation grew worse when one evening, as I was leaving my office, which was downstairs in the gloomy and dark basement, I noticed the general's daughter making a mess in their kitchen. She was a teenager, and I could tell she was spoiled. Nearby their crazy Labrador retriever was also making a mess. They always expected me to clean up after that damn dog, gathering its hair on a daily basis and picking up its shit. The next day when I came in, the kitchen looked ridiculous, as if a food fight had taken place in it. I didn't clean it up, since it wasn't my mess to deal with. Not long after I came in, I received a call on my office phone.

"Sergeant Rush. What happened?"

I clutched the receiver. "What happened with what?"

"What happened last night? The general said that you left a mess."

"I'm sorry?"

"The general said that you left a mess," the chief of staff stated.

"That's a negative. I didn't leave any mess."

This guy knew me. He knew my work habits and my personal code. He had known me for a long time and knew how I operated with everybody. He knew all my records and evaluations and promotions and *everything*. But here's the deal: even though he knew me, he also knew his rank and he knew he could never stand up for me. He understood that even though the general was wrong, he still had to accuse me of making this mess. That's just the way it works.

"So then what happened?" he asked again.

I didn't explain that it was their daughter because I didn't need to. "I'm telling you it wasn't me. I don't know what you're talking about."

"So then why would the general say this?"

"I don't give a fuck," I said. "I just told you it wasn't fucking me. You know my character and how I do my job. You know this wasn't me. So why the fuck are you telling me this again?"

"Someone has to clean it up," the chief of staff said.

"I'm not a fucking servant," I said, hanging up the phone.

I knew I was all out of ranks, how I was crossing a line. I knew how close to the edge I had gotten, how much I had been pushing things, how my PTSD was beginning to impact everything else.

You're working twenty-four hours a day and when you come home you sit on the couch and just rock away. You're not eating and not sleeping and you're alone every day.

Shortly after this, I heard steps coming down to my office. I was sitting at my desk facing my computer when the general's voice boomed from behind me.

"Sergeant Rush, do you know who I am?"

"Sir," I said, gritting my teeth, still facing forward.

"I said do you know who I am?"

The voice was right behind me, breathing down on me with its contempt and scorn. I was sitting there and I felt my entire body begin to shake. Every sense inside of me was firing off, and I had to use all of my strength to stay in my chair.

"Do you know who—"

Before he finished his sentence, I jumped out of my chair and I swung around, only to see his frightened face and his tall figure backing off.

"*That's* who you are," I said.

I ran up the stairs, taking my fury with me. I left the house with my emotions caged inside and my career still intact. I knew if I had touched the general, I would have been sent to Leavenworth, the United States Penitentiary. I would have been finished. I climbed into my car and drove off, taking my anger and hostility with me as traveling companions. I still had to think about the future.

I'm just a black man in the military. It doesn't matter what I've done, I'm still a black man. If I touch the general, I'm finished.

I drove back to my place, and when I got inside, I did the one thing I've never done. It was like the time I asked my father to borrow money for the car. The first and the last time I ever did that. I decided to pick up the phone and make a call to ask for a favor. I never asked for anything despite knowing so many people. People told me all the time, "Chef, if you ever need anything, just ask." I always told them no, and I always told myself the same thing. But today was a first. I called a general I knew who had a higher rank than the asshole I was working for. I explained the entire situation starting from the beginning.

"Chef, don't worry about it," the general said. "Come back to DC."

I had been planning on going back anyway, but I had stayed at West Point for the new general, and he had stopped anything more from happening. So all this time I was waiting go to DC, and at the same time I was working Sergeant Durden hard, really putting him through his paces.

Everything changed when he received premature orders to leave and go back to his last place of duty.

★   ★   ★

I needed to ask someone for another favor. Every ounce of me didn't want to do it, but I was desperate. This was an emergency. I had to go to my principal at West Point.

Sergeant Durden had come here for compassionate reassignment and was supposed to stay for at least twelve months, but now he had orders to leave. That meant he was going back to Fort Bragg. The moment I heard him tell me that, I knew he was in trouble.

"Fuck—you can't go back to Fort Bragg," I said.

"I know. I told my therapist and she said I'm not supposed to go, that I still have therapy to do, that they'll vouch for me. They will say I'm not done with my treatment."

"I'm going to talk to the general," I told him.

I had to do the unthinkable.

I'm going to fucking do the one thing I hate—the one thing I never, ever want to do. I'm going to get on my fucking knees and beg him to let the sergeant stay here.

That is what leaders do. More importantly, that's what friends do. They make tough choices when faced with life-and-death circumstances.

I took the long walk and said I needed to speak to the general, so I was let in. I stood in front of this man I hated, standing at attention in my parade stance. He already knew why I was there.

"Sir, they want Sergeant Durden to go back to Fort Bragg," I said. "You know what happened there, sir, the journey he's been on. The therapist says he needs more time. Sir, he needs to stay here as long as possible. Please, sir."

The cold stare of the general didn't show any emotion. "Go bring him in. Let me talk to him."

"Thank you, sir. Thank you."

I was excited when I got Sergeant Durden and drove him over to the general myself. I waited outside the general's office as the sergeant went in for the meeting, but I didn't have to wait long. When Durden walked back out, he wore a big smile. A huge weight dropped off my shoulders and I let out a silent *phew*.

"So he's going to let you stay?" I asked.

"No," Sergeant Durden said.

"What? So why the fuck are you smiling?"

He showed me something in his hand.

"Because he gave me this cool coin and told me—"

I slapped the coin out of Durden's hand before he could finish his sentence.

"*That's* why you're smiling? For real?"

"It's okay," the sergeant told me with no ounce of concern on his bright face.

"No, it's not," I said, feeling the weight of the situation press back on me. "It's not okay."

★   ★   ★

So this was the reason why I wasn't okay with Sergeant Durden going back to Fort Bragg.

While the soldier was serving his country in Iraq, his wife and two children were stationed at the military installation in North Carolina. One night, a soldier on base broke into the Durden household while the family was there. They said he was drunk. He was also a predator, because he knew the sergeant's wife was there alone. The man raped Durden's wife repeatedly in front of their kids, telling her if she didn't let him, he would kill them.

Immediately after discovering what happened, the Army grabbed Sergeant Durden and brought him back from Iraq to New York. His wife and children were brought there as well. This was why he was on compassionate reassignment, and why he had broken down telling me his story and sharing how happy he was to be working under me. He had begun to heal through his therapy. I constantly talked to him and inspired him and coached him and encouraged him and pushed him. I accompanied the sergeant when they finally had a court date, and I stood by him when they sentenced the rapist to prison.

When it came time for me to say goodbye to Durden, I wept. All this training and growth and now he was leaving. He was going back to a place he needed to stay far away from. He didn't have the same support system there at Fort Bragg, and the asshole I worked for knew that. The general knew all the grisly details, yet he was content to send the sergeant and his family back. As I cried saying goodbye, the sergeant consoled me.

"It's gonna be okay, Master Sergeant," he said.

Sergeant Durden wasn't just my soldier. He was my little brother, my blood.

We don't put on this uniform and say, "I'll see you later." It's always just "I see you."

★　★　★

When the sergeant and his family were back at Fort Bragg, I checked in with him on a regular basis. I'd text him to see what was the latest happening in his life.

How's it going, youngblood? Any word on the job yet?

Not yet, bro, Durden would write back. *Just playing around, playing the waiting game. LOL! How are you doing?*

He sounded fine and normal like he always did. I was concerned more about *how* he was doing than about *what* he was doing.

One day when I was with a bunch of military guys, training them like I always did, my cell phone rang and I could see Durden was calling. I decided to give him a call back that evening, since we spoke all the time. The day was long, and by the time I could give Durden a call, it was late, and I knew I had to get up early in the morning to go to Fort Eustis, an Army installation in Virginia that was around three hours away. Since I would be getting up in just a few hours, I decided to call the sergeant back tomorrow.

After leaving at 3:00 a.m. on my trip, I had been driving for an hour before getting a phone call. It was a strange number but I knew immediately where it was from. It was from Iraq.

Why the fuck is someone calling me from Iraq?

When I answered, one of the guys I knew greeted me. He was a sergeant.

"Hey, Sergeant Rush. I have something to tell you."

"What's that?"

"It's about Sergeant Durden."

"Yeah, he called me last night. I'm going to give him a call today. Why? Is he back in Iraq? I just spoke to him."

I was joking around, not thinking anything about the call. The voice on the other end didn't sound amused or in the mood to joke around.

"I wanted to call you because I know how much you meant to Sergeant Durden. And I know what you did for him."

"Tell me what?" I asked.

"Sergeant Durden committed suicide."

"What the fuck are you talking about?" I said. "He just called me. He didn't commit suicide."

"Yes, Sergeant. He did."

I refused to believe this nonsense, to even begin to comprehend what this meant.

"Get me the report," I told him.

I still had two hours to drive, so I rolled the windows down and blasted music and tried to keep whatever hope I could that this sergeant was misinformed, that there was some mistake. I focused on the soldiers I was about to meet and train while blocking out the reality that I'd just learned about. But nothing I could do could outrun the bitter truth.

Right before I arrived at Fort Eustis, I got another phone call from the sergeant in Iraq telling me he emailed me the report. I pulled into a parking lot and read what had happened. Sergeant Durden was on Fort Bragg and had killed himself with a shotgun in his car. Before I had any time to process this, my cell phone buzzed and I saw it was Sergeant Durden's wife calling. She was calling to tell me the news, assuming I didn't know.

"Sergeant Rush, I want to tell you that Durden passed away last night."

She didn't say suicide. I didn't tell her I knew.

"The family knows how much you meant to him," she told me. "We want you to come back to Fort Bragg to do the eulogy."

"Of course I will. I will be there."

★   ★   ★

When I arrived at the funeral a few days later, I kept a steadfast face as I greeted Sergeant Durden's mother and father. They gave me hugs as they stood in front of the closed casket for my soldier. Next to the casket were two soldiers in uniform, standing at attention and not saying anything. They were there to say, "We're here to support our fallen brother."

I had arrived right before the funeral was about to start, and as I was speaking to the sergeant's parents, an ornate arrangement of flowers were delivered. Mr. and Mrs. Durden asked who the flowers were from, and when the name was spoken, I felt my stomach drop and my blood begin to boil. I breathed in slowly.

"Sir, ma'am?" I said to them. "Could you please do me a favor?"

"What is it?" they asked.

"Those flowers that you just received. Could you not bring them into the funeral service?"

The sergeant's parents said that was okay and didn't ask me why. They couldn't understand that these flowers came from the general who helped contribute to Sergeant Durden's death. A top general in the military who was supposed to take up for all soldiers and military members who were in need. A leader who was supposed to help those underneath him who were in distress.

I hated that general. I blamed that general. But at the same time, I also blamed myself in part, even though I didn't realize it at the time. Sergeant Durden's death would never leave me, and his passing would not be in vain. Some sort of good had to come from this.

★ ★ ★

Even though I left West Point and went to DC immediately after this happened, that wasn't the end of the story between the general and me. I did the best thing I could do, utilizing my sources and reaching out to people to get in touch with me. Eventually people from the Inspector General Department of Defense (IGDOD) approached me and asked to talk to me. They were from an independent agency that gives oversight to programs and operations in the Department of Defense. These guys were at a high level.

I didn't hesitate to talk to them. I did what I had never done and what I never do. I spoke out. "So this is what's going on . . ." I decided to tell them what this toxic leader did. *He did this* and *he did that* and *he also did this*, and all the while these guys at the IGDOD were in disbelief that I was actually telling them.

The truth about this general needed to be known. I could deal with his disdain and disregard for me. I could put up with his disrespect, how he demeaned me and my role. I didn't care if he was racist or emasculating or both. I could cook for his wife and be content with regifted Starbucks gift cards. I could clean up after his insane dog who pissed and shed hair everywhere. I did all those things and I was fine to leave and say nothing, but the situation with Sergeant Durden's death was different.

After an internal investigation, Pentagon investigators found that the general had misused his office by doing unethical things that were against policy and procedures. They had even held the general back from his retirement because they were doing the investigation. The inspector general recommended the Army consider taking corrective action against the general, and the Army officially admonished him for his improper actions. They never mentioned my name in the report because they didn't have to, but I didn't care. I didn't care. They thought they were protecting me, but I told them I didn't give a shit.

They needed to know something about me.

I can be your biggest ally or your worst fucking enemy. I'm a black man—no, I'm a man who has nothing except respect. But you're not gonna disrespect me. You let a fucking soldier go down.

I was proud of what I did. From that alone, the Army changed regulations on how the enlisted were to be treated in similar situations. But none of that mattered.

None of that could bring back Sergeant Durden.

HEART AND BODY

We forget nothing really. But so long as we have to stay here in
the field, the front-line days, when they are past, sink down in us
like a stone; they are too grievous for us to be able to reflect on
them at once. If we did that, we should have been destroyed long
ago. I soon found out this much: terror can be endured so long as
a man simply ducks;—but it kills, if a man thinks about it.

ALL QUIET ON THE WESTERN FRONT, ERICH MARIA REMARQUE

"We're going to need to scope your shoulders."
  I gave the doctor a puzzled look. "Do I really
need that? I know they're in a lot of pain, but that
seems extreme."
  In 2010, I went to the military hospital because my shoulder
was in constant pain and was told that the scope was a necessity.
Since I'm a very trusting type of person, I went ahead with the
scope. *It's the military, for God's sake,* I thought at the time. I had
no idea what they were about to do to me.
  When I woke up from surgery, I discovered that they had cut
off and reattached my bicep without even bothering to ask me.

Since the biceps tendon attaches directly into the shoulder joint, some surgeons perform a procedure called biceps tenodesis to deal with shoulder pain when they see that a biceps tendon has damage. This procedure involves detaching the biceps tendon and then implanting it back on top of the arm bone. This makes the biceps weaker, so it doesn't grow as much. The procedure is also done with a pin, so the biceps can tear easier.

Nobody ever considered waking me up to ask whether I wanted to have biceps fucking tenodesis. Instead, they just cut away and told me after the fact.

"You needed it," the doctors and nurses explained.

"I needed it? Why?"

I never got a clear answer. They explained that my condition was most likely hereditary, and then they asked about my family members and who had what. They explained how my shoulders would never fully regain their strength and that they couldn't grow back.

I felt violated, and this violation went even deeper than muscles and bones. This went to my psyche and my soul. I stopped wearing tank tops or anything close to resembling them. I became self-conscious, even though the muscles grew back and I had no reason to feel any sort of self-doubt. But this is what wounds and scars can do to you. Even when they heal, you can carry them hidden and out of sight. It's only been in the past year that I've started to get over this phobia. That's what happens when people cut you open and operate on you without asking.

★　★　★

There are no excuses.

Let me rephrase that. There are no fucking excuses. None.

People don't understand that when they see this body, they don't know about all the scars and tears it has taken. They don't realize that I've had both my biceps cut off and reattached. That I've had both of my shoulders opened up for irrelevant surgeries and then told that they would never grow again. People can't fathom how fucking hard it's been for me to get this physique after everything I've gone through.

Then again, I do have to admit that my body isn't like other people's bodies. Another story that illustrates this is when I almost died while I was still working at West Point.

As I've said, I was working all the time. I was visiting Fort Lee to speak to a class there, so I got off work and made the eight-hour drive from New York to Virginia. I arrived on a Wednesday, spoke on Thursday, and Friday I went to DC. While I was there, I began to feel really weird and didn't know why. I felt lethargic and dizzy, and I couldn't go to the restroom. I became so sick that I decided to go to the Fort Belvoir hospital's emergency room. They put me on a gurney and made me wait a long time, then they hooked me up to an IV and began checking me out. After a few hours, they gave me some medication while three doctors spoke about my diagnosis. Two of them were white and one was black, which is ironic since the first two said that it was okay to go ahead and release me, but the other said he didn't think they should. He felt like they should keep me in the ER. You can guess what happened.

I was on my way out of the hospital when I ended up passing out. When I got back into the ICU, all hell broke loose with my liver and my lungs and my kidneys—everything in my body. I had a fever spiking to 104. It was fucking crazy. In those first seventy-two hours, the doctors could not figure out what was wrong. They did everything from a spinal tap without medication to soaking me in a bathtub full of ice to get my temperature down. I lost my vision for a while. At one point I looked up and saw that my temperature had spiked to 108. The nurses were saying, "No, no, that can't be right."

For three days I was in so much agony, with every part of my body hurting. I remember vague impressions of those days. At one point, a doctor asked me if I had just been in an earthquake. There I was in an ICU in Virginia, and I'm thinking, *Why the fuck would you ask me that question?* I later found out that sometimes during earthquakes, your body can be shocked into rhabdomyolysis and leak toxins. On the third day, a preacher came in and sat by my bed to read me my last rites. That's how bad the situation had become. I heard the doctors at one point saying, "He's not going to make it." And honestly, I was ready to go. But the very next day after hearing that, my fever broke. I stayed at the hospital for four more weeks as I recovered.

Here's how fucking selfish I was: When they thought I was going to die and asked me if I wanted to contact anybody, I told them no. I didn't tell my mother or my sisters or anybody that I was in the ER literally on my deathbed. It was dumb, but I didn't want anybody to be with me, not in that condition.

Now, I could have been taken to a major hospital—I should've been taken to one—but these doctors knew who I was, so they kept me at this smaller hospital. They wanted me there because of who I worked for. My principal at West Point, the one who wanted me picking up his dog's hair rather than performing my regular duties, came to visit me. It was an awkward visit; the general acted as if this was something he needed to do.

When the doctors released me, they told me not to drive or do anything. So naturally I got into my car and drove back to New York. It's supposed to be a five-hour trip, but in my condition it took me ten hours because I had to stop so many times.

I hobbled back to my place, feeling weak and out of it. I decided to go to the small hospital by me at West Point, and they immediately sent me to a major hospital. I knew a doctor who was out of town, at this larger hospital, so I went to see him.

"Chef . . . what's wrong with you?"

I informed him what had happened and how nobody knew what was wrong with me. The doctor did all the normal things, taking my temperature and my blood pressure and other tests, and he soon told me he was admitting me back to the ICU.

"I can't," I told him. "I got to get back to work."

The doctor looked at me like I was a crazy man. "Do you want to die?"

"I'll tell you after work," I said.

I wasn't being funny; that was my plan as I walked out of the hospital and climbed into my car to drive off. The MPs (military police) had to come get me and bring me back to the hospital. But this was my mindset.

No excuses. No defeat. Nothing's taking me down.

Well, whatever this was, it took me down again while I was laid up in the ICU. I crashed again and remained in there for another six weeks. They performed tests on me like I was some lab rat—every test in the world—but there were still no results. Nobody knew what happened.

When I could finally walk again, they sent me back home with orders to take the pills they were giving me. Everybody who saw me looked mortified, like they were seeing some sort of ghost. I hadn't seen myself in weeks, so when I stepped in the bathroom for the first time to take a shower, I took off my clothes and stood in front of a mirror. As I stared at the stranger in front of me, I started to laugh.

"God giveth and God taketh away," I said out loud as I chuckled.

I was skin and bones. I mean—I was nothing. I couldn't remember the last time I ever looked like this. Maybe never.

Two weeks later, I went in for a checkup with my doctor, and the moment he looked at me, he gasped.

"What the hell did you do?" he said.

I understood his shock. Everything—my whole entire body—had come back. The muscles, the size, everything shot back up as if I had never gotten sick. He called in other doctors to examine me. Like this mysterious illness, nobody could figure out what had just happened with my body, including me.

"Chef," the doctor said, "I don't know what your regimen is or what you were doing or what you did. But you shouldn't be here."

I ended up doing dozens of tests and talking to every specialist there was—Army, military, civilian—and nobody could determine what exactly happened. To this day it's still a mystery: what happened and when it happened and how it happened.

My body had come back stronger and bigger than it was. It came back *better*. It came back like it had just been attacked. It had fucking won and it wanted to celebrate.

★   ★   ★

Imagine having a superpower and all of a sudden someone takes it away. Imagine people thinking that your arms are the strongest things that you have, but it's actually your legs. It's actually your running. It's actually your speed. And then someone takes it away. That's what happened to me.

One of the most serious injuries I've ever had occurred when my quadriceps ruptured. Unfortunately, it was another mishap exacerbated by the military, an injury that could have improved if people hadn't been so damn ignorant.

Ever since I was a kid, I've been sensitive about wearing shorts. That's because when I young, I had a bad case of chicken pox, and since I had my mother's lighter-skinned complexion, the chicken pox gave me dark bruises on my legs that I hid. They eventually went away, but to me, they are still there.

Going back to my high school days when they wanted me to wrestle, I've always loved to fight. To train how to fight. While I was at West Point, I was a combative trainer. This was another release for me, the same way cooking was. One day while I was fighting with the guys, I felt my quadriceps blow up. I knew my body well enough to know this was a rupture. Right away I went into the emergency room on the military base. After being there six or seven hours, they told me it was nothing but a strain.

"A strain?" I asked them in disbelief. "Do you see my leg? A strain?"

My leg had swollen to twice the size of my arm. Maybe even bigger. It wasn't a fucking strain.

"We would give you crutches, but we don't have any," they said, adding insult to injury. "Do you have a set?"

I hobbled out of the ER angry and knowing they were wrong. I did have some crutches, so I hobbled around on them for a week, then another and another, all while my leg continued to get worse. I was working in DC for a general. By week four, the general noticed something was seriously wrong.

"Chef, something's going on here," he told me. You're feeble. I am going to call a surgeon general. We're going to get you checked out."

The next day when they did an MRI, they told me what I already knew. My quadriceps was indeed ruptured and my whole leg was fucked up and done.

"Chef, you need surgery tomorrow," the doctor told me without any reservation. "We need to do surgery immediately. This is really bad. You can lose your leg."

All I could think was, *Fucking military doctors*. Of course, my dumb ass said, "No, I have work to do." I've said this a few times during life-threatening situations.

"Can you give me five days?" I asked the surgeon. "I gotta go do an event."

"Are you serious?" he said.

"Yeah. I have to go to Fort Lee for this culinary show."

So my dumb ass with this busted leg needing surgery drove all the way to Fort Lee to do this event that I've done for years, the first event in which I competed with other chefs. This culinary show was done once a year with all the military across all branches and all over the world. I went there now to train military personnel who wouldn't have this opportunity anywhere else.

One thing I taught the newcomers was the attitude I brought with me everywhere. I will never forget the first time I went to this show, when I didn't know shit about anything but learned from seeing others do it. In the beginning, every time I competed, I would get in front of these guys who had all this experience, look at them with complete confidence, then say, "You ready to lose?" They always had the same expressions that said, *What the fuck is wrong with this kid? Are you ready to lose?* But I also made them wonder about me, thinking that maybe there was something going on that they didn't know.

I told the guys I was training at Fort Lee that even though I did lose in those first competitions, it didn't matter, because I had to be my biggest fan. I had to ignore those who doubted me. I showed up without any experience, so simply being there was a victory. It was just like what I told Sergeant Durden: you win because you're there. Speaking of winning, even with my busted leg I did an ice carving at the show. Our three-man team won a gold.

When I came back from Fort Lee, I got the surgery, and it was fucking terrible. I went to Fort Meade, which was an improvement, and I had a great doctor who worked on me. When they opened my leg up, it was worse than they imagined. The muscle had atrophied, since it had been so much time since I first went into the ER for the injury.

Ultimately the bones needed to be fused and cadaver tissue placed in my leg. After the fusion, it felt like my leg had a steel rod or a two-by-four inserted into it. My doctor agreed that the people who had said this was only a strain were idiots.

"That's poor service to our military members," he said. "They were just being lazy. That could have cost you a leg."

Unfortunately, that's the situation in the military too many times. It's happened before.

Right after my surgery, I got two phone calls. The sort of life-changing phone calls you don't want to get when you're down to one leg. One of them was an assignment with the Delta Force. I couldn't believe it. I fucking love Delta. Once I had an opportunity to go, but others had denied me for some reason. Delta is different from the rest of the military. They take care of their own. Their missions are secret. Delta Force is its own world, and that's what I loved about it. You didn't decide to join Delta—they chose you. They were some of the Army's best soldiers and leaders. The unit is primarily used for counterterrorism when needing to kill or capture the enemy and to dismantle terrorist cells. People always said, once you join Delta, you will become them and lose everyone around you. They didn't know that I already had.

I hated passing on Delta Force, but another opportunity came around the same time. I received another call from a general I knew.

"Hey, Chef, I want you to come to Iraq."

"You want me to come to Iraq?"

Obviously, he didn't know about my busted leg.

"Yes. We are going to be here for two years."

"I'm in," my dumb ass said without a further thought.

They were already on the ground in Iraq, so they asked me how quickly I could come. Part of me knew I couldn't even think about going, not with my leg in the shape it was in. But I was determined to go.

When I went to physical therapy after the surgery, I knew the therapist from all my previous injuries over the years. As she examined my charts, she looked shocked.

"Wow—what happened?"

I honestly can't tell you how bad my leg happened to be. First I explained to her what happened, and she couldn't get over how horrific it looked. Then when I told the physical therapist my situation and the plans I had to leave for Iraq, she said the same thing my doctors and other therapists said.

"You're not going anywhere."

"No, no, I'm on orders," I said. "I gotta go to Iraq."

My mentality was *I have to go back to Iraq. I gotta fucking serve my country. I gotta do this.* Looking back, I know this is a portrait of stupidity and stubbornness, but it's also a picture of resiliency and resolve.

"Chef, you know what? I'll humor you," my physical therapist said.

"Okay, humor me."

"This will never happen, but if you can get your leg to move into a ninety-degree angle in thirty days, I will let you go."

"Ninety degrees in thirty days?" I laughed. "Seriously?"

"That's the only way."

I began to do the math. I was meeting with her two times a week, so that meant eight sessions in therapy. The first week, my leg didn't move. Not an inch, not even five degrees. Every day I woke up, the pain remained by my side and stayed there all day long. By the second week, I began to be able to move it slightly. I saw my therapist more often, sometimes every other day, continuing to tell her I needed to go to Iraq and continuing to hear her explain it wasn't going to happen.

This sort of injury takes six months to heal. That didn't matter. I needed to make this happen. One evening, I got two bath towels and a washcloth. I looped the two towels together and stuck one end underneath the foot of my injured leg, then I wrapped that with duct tape to make sure the foot remained in position. I placed the washcloth between my teeth and began to pull my leg, trying to get it to budge. I had to break the bone and cartilage in the leg. It was the most excruciating pain I could imagine. It was a tie between this and when I almost died in the hospital. The difference was this was self-inflicted. This pain was coming from me.

Some days I spent most of the day doing this, pulling my foot and trying to make it bend. When it had been thirty days, I went in to the therapist and she began to test my leg to see how far it could bend. Sure enough, she got to seventy degrees no problem, then seventy-five, eighty, and all the time I'm grimacing and sweating. Eighty-five. Then barely . . . finally . . . ninety degrees.

Amazingly, I was cleared to go to Iraq.

To this very day, my leg still hurts like crazy. Sometimes I get angry about it because it never should have happened.

My legs were the strongest part of me, even stronger than my arms. They were fast and tough and made me a star track athlete. Hell, they earned me the nickname Horse. Now one of my legs was gone. I grew up as a runner, a big runner, and I was always working out with my legs. Legs were my passion.

When I had my leg injury, a part of me was taken away forever.

It was a terrible situation, but the memory and the ache are reminders. Not only of how bad things can happen when you least expect them, but of how a person can overcome those situations. How somebody can endure an injury like this and set his mind to do something nobody expects.

Bending my leg and being cleared to go to Iraq was the first step. Now the tough part would be getting there.

★　★　★

Nobody in the Army knew about my busted leg as I made my trek from the US to Iraq carrying four hundred-pound rucksacks with me. Nobody could see the brace on my knee or the slight limp in my walk. I didn't tell anybody and didn't show any signs of stress. I didn't ask for anything—I was just trying to do my job. There I was, carrying those massive duffel bags with one in each hand, one in back, and another in front, going through the holding area and onto the transport and the flight and then helicopters, the weight pressing down on my weak leg. Every fucking step made me want to scream, but I held it all inside. I knew if I told anybody, their perspective on me would change.

When I finally arrived at the base in Baghdad, I was relieved. I would be working with the general there and my room was close to his, meaning if any sort of attack were to occur, I would be the first line of defense if someone got through the guards we had in the front.

The first day I got there, I met the chaplain's assistant, who became a good friend of mine. I was starving, so we went to the dining hall, and the food they were serving that day was Indian food. I love Indian food, and this was delicious, so I had ten plates of it. Just inhaling it, stuffing myself.

It was the worst thing I could have ever done.

On that first day after making this numbingly painful trip to Iraq, only hours after arriving at the base, I got the worst bout of food poisoning imaginable. This wasn't your average food poisoning; this was the mother of it because this didn't make you go to the bathroom or throw up. This sort of food poisoning just made you sit there feeling miserable while it refused to go anywhere. *I'm not coming out of your mouth or your ass,* it said. *I'm just going to be here.* I've never had food poisoning like that. There was no relief or letup. I couldn't believe it either. I had to check in and had all these duties I needed to perform, and I got food poisoning? So for that first week, I was walking misery. I felt terrible.

Things began shaky, but it felt great to be back in Iraq. I was back to a place where I felt like I belonged, being part of something few others could experience. I was part of a team, part of a mission. There's nothing like being in a place that is about survival. Your senses and your relationships and your routines— everything becomes amplified when you're in this sort of place where you depend on someone and someone depends on you. You become bonded forever with these people as you make memories that won't ever be forgotten. You also get to learn who you really are all over again.

I had been working in a toxic environment those last few years at West Point. Now I was back on the field, feeling the dirt and the sweat on my skin. I had always loved to crawl around in the mud and get dirty. I didn't realize when I went over to Iraq that I needed to go there for me, I needed to go there for my country, and I needed to go there to do what I needed to do. I needed to go there for so many different reasons.

My job was to serve underneath the commander for the base, who was in charge of the whole operation. If anything happened, he would be the main target. We worked so much it was crazy. The general would stay up for twenty-four hours. We would start some days at 3:00 a.m. and then finally go to bed at 10:00 or 11:00 p.m., then do it all over again. It might sound insane, but this was so liberating; even when I was put in danger, when hearing those sirens. It's impossible to sum up everything that happened during this time—so much occurred. There were attacks and people got killed.

I remember one of the Navy guys on the base showed up gashed and bleeding. He said an Iraqi came on the base and attacked him. No one could figure out how the Iraqi got on the base in the first place. It turned out this guy had cut himself because he wanted to get a medal. When they found this out, the Navy guy had to stay there until we got rid of him, and it became like the walk of shame everywhere this guy went.

Everybody came there for different reasons, and the place had different effects on each person. For me, I wanted to get away and do what I came to do.

I didn't know that I was still carrying all the trauma from the last few years with me, and that at some point, I would be forced to confront it.

★   ★   ★

"Hey, Andre. You can relax a little bit."

The general was getting ready to take the bird and head off the base when he told me this. We had been working seven days a week for ten months. It was a month before I was scheduled to leave Iraq and go back home. I told him okay and headed to my room.

In the silence, I stared at the ceiling, at the walls around me. The grief I'd been trying to outrun had caught up to me.

I still saw Sergeant Durden's smile and heard his laugh. I remember a time—some random conversation—when we were in the kitchen joking and working, and he mentioned the news that someone we knew had committed suicide. I will never forget his words.

"Man, I'd never do that," Durden told me. "That's just crazy."

It *is* crazy. Any senseless death is crazy. Especially his.

So many things raced through my mind, things I'd managed to outrun until then. This giant blanket of pain and hate and loss and longing covered me. I hadn't processed Durden's death. Then again, there was so much shit I hadn't even started to try to process. The asshole general. 9/11.

You've been running for a long time, Horse.

You never forget trauma. You might bury those painful memories and emotions, but they never leave you. They hang on your soul like medals decorating your suffering.

I knew I needed some sleep. I never slept. I remembered I had two bottles of Ambien. So in my bed, with all these different things spinning in my head, all I wanted was to go to sleep for a very long time. Before I knew it, I was opening up the sleeping pills and taking them. Taking them all. I had been alone for the last few years, and now that we were getting ready to leave Iraq, I just wanted to be left alone. Even being there in this place with all those people, at least I knew I wouldn't be bothered. The general wasn't going to be back. I took all the pills and drifted off to rest.

I wanted to sleep, but my body wanted to fight. My fucking body . . .

All of a sudden, I opened my eyes, then moved in a lethargic state and rolled off the bed. I opened my eyes and stared around the room. I felt like shit and began to gag. I knew how fucked up I was. I crawled to the bathroom, where there was a make-shift shower, and I turned the water on even though I was still in my clothes. As the water doused me, I tried to gag myself so I could vomit up the sleeping pills.

With the steady stream of cold water hitting me, I was flooded with everything. My entire life gushed out of that faucet onto the writhing figure on the ground that was me.

They say you have to die to be reborn. Maybe that's what was happening to me.

I didn't feel as though I was under the water but rather experienced being above it looking down on myself. I knew I was by myself in the compound, so nobody could get in. Nobody could knock on the door and come in and try to help me. No one would know what was happening unless they came looking for me, and that was not happening because the general and his aide were gone. So there I was lying in the bottom of the shower, soaked and feeling like shit, and my body decided to speak up. This was what my body said:

"I'm hungry."

Really? I just made myself sick, and this is what the fuck you tell me?

It seems like every time I'm in a life-or-death situation, my body tells me what to do.

After barely making it to Iraq with my broken body, I almost didn't make it back to the States. My body was still intact, but my spirit was shattered in a million different parts. I needed help, but was too stubborn to ask for it.

PTSD IS REAL

When I returned to West Point after coming back home from Iraq, everything was different. I was different. I didn't smile and didn't want to talk to others. I could feel the toxicity in the air. It was almost as if I was smelling the poison surrounding me.

Even before leaving Iraq, that dread related to my former general at West Point returned. He was in New York, and that was where I would be going when I returned to the US My general in Iraq called me in one day and informed me about a video call he had with the colonel at West Point.

"Andre, I just got off VTC with the chief of staff, and the general said you need to walk on eggshells when you come back."

What the fuck?

My general knew about what had happened at West Point with my former principal and with Sergeant Durden.

"Andre, what do you think about that?" the general asked.

"Sir. Honestly?" I laughed. "Here you have this general—one of the highest of the highs—at one of greatest and most powerful military academies in the world. And here he is thousands and thousands of miles away, tens of thousands of miles away, telling his colonel to deliver a message to me. This general wants to tell a measly old master sergeant that I need to walk on eggshells. Sir, I am going to tell you something. It's pathetic to actually hear this."

The general nodded but warned me again. "Andre, just be careful. Don't go around him."

"Sir, don't you worry about that. I'm not going to do anything."

I realized when I got back to West Point that I was starting over again with different leaders and different people who felt they like they were very, very important. I hate wagon jumpers, those sort of people who jump on everybody's ass, and the colonel who left a message for my general was one of them. He was a piece of shit, and it was difficult for me to not say this to his face. The others around him were the same way. I was doing the same thing I always did—taking charge—but every time I disagreed with someone, they felt like I was being aggressive. Actually, I wasn't being aggressive until they forced me to be.

One day while I was driving on the campus of West Point, a man in a convertible pulled out right in front of me and almost crashed head-on into me. When I heard this moron honk his horn as if it were my fault, I went crazy. My anger came out of the blue. I jumped out of my car and rushed over to the guy.

"Get out of the fucking car," I yelled at him.

He didn't move, so I said it again.

"Why am I gonna get out of my car?" he asked. "You're just gonna whup my ass."

He backed up and drove off, and while he did, I took in what just happened.

Dre, man . . . you're losing it.

I had almost gotten into accidents before and had seen people do some stupid things on the road, but I had never jumped out of my car and confronted someone. So why did I do it this time?

You've changed, Dre.

I knew it, but I refused to believe it. With the new general there, everybody wanted to kiss his ass while at the same time everyone wanted to be in charge. I had been in this situation before, and I knew what I was doing. *I'm the same person I am all the time,* I reasoned. *Everybody else has changed.* Every single time I had to do something, everyone wanted to flex on me. Just because of who I was and how I looked, they all thought I was being aggressive. In retrospect, I can see they were being disrespected. When someone told me to do something, I would tell them, "Negative," saying it was not in the best interests of the superintendent, as regulations permit. If someone asked the general to do something and I told him the opposite, people got upset. This continued to happen, and something needed to give.

One day the general I served in Iraq called me into his office. He had known me for years, and I loved him and his wife. I had come back to West Point to serve him as the superintendent. We had a great working relationship; I was his soldier, and he was my boss, but we were also friends. That didn't change the fact that he outranked me.

"How's it going?" the general asked.

"It's going well, sir."

I asked him what was going on and why he wanted to see me.

"You know, Andre," the general said, sitting back with his arms crossed, "I think it's about that time."

"It's time for what, sir?"

"You know. It's that time."

I still wasn't following. "Time for what?"

"Andre, you have served your country diligently. Now it's time for us to take care of you."

"Sir. What the hell does that mean?"

He just sat there. I knew what that meant.

"Sir . . .," I said, and then in an instant the dam burst open. "Do you know who I am? Do you know what I've done? You can't fucking crack my code. I fucking held this goddamn temple for fucking goddamn twenty fucking years. I've held all this shit in—all these things. I was fucking steadfast the whole fucking time. Nobody cracks my fucking code. Nobody fucking does that. I've done the fucking best job at the worst times in the worst situations and the most unspeakable times. And you're telling me that I need help, sir?"

He still sat back in his chair, not reacting to my words and emotion. I stood up and exited, and when I got back to my quarters the phone rang.

"Master Sergeant," someone said. "You have an appointment tomorrow at 9:00 a.m."

"Roger," I said.

The general knew I was losing it. Everybody, in fact, knew I was losing it. The principal knew that if the day came when I truly lost it, things could end up turning ugly for me and my military career. He believed somebody might try to do something to trigger me deliberately. Or it might be as simple as some moron deciding to get out of his car to confront me.

The following morning, I went to see the therapist on the fourth floor of a building. He talked to me about therapy, his words going in one ear and right back out of the other. I said all the things I needed to say and acted the way I needed to act.

After making my next appointment, I walked down the slender hallway to the elevator in full disbelief, wondering what the fuck I was doing there. A big white guy walked the other way and looked straight at me. I knew he was in the special forces. We both gave each other knowing glances. I passed him by and got to the elevator while the big guy went to the counter.

Just before the elevator doors opened, I heard footsteps running toward me. When I looked, I saw the big guy standing right in front of me.

"Brother," he said, "I know if you're here, I need to be here."

We gave each other a big hug. After I got into the elevator, I exhaled because I knew.

I'm never putting my head down again in this place. If that's the response I get, then that's the response I always want.

I wasn't ready for treatment, but I was walking the path that led me to recovery. I just had a long road to travel. Of course, there would be some detours too. The sort of detours that change your life forever.

★　★　★

"Andre, you need to come home and see your brother."

When my sister called and told me I needed to go see Ricky, I immediately gave her all the typical excuses. I was busy and I had plans and I needed to do this and that. None of them mattered.

"No, Andre. You need to come home and see your brother."

I knew something was serious, so I told my sister I would come.

Ricky was seventeen years older than me. When our family moved out from the projects into a small house, Ricky went to live on a farm. I loved visiting him there and seeing the horses and ducks and cows in the pasture. I used to go out and chase the rabbits. They were fast, but I eventually got to the point where I could grab them by the ears. That's when I realized just how fast I happened to be.

Ricky had always been more of an outdoorsman. When he was younger, he had been in the merchant marines, but he came back, married, and had my nephews and nieces. I grew up watching Ricky fishing. He was a natural, catching catfish and bringing them around. Ricky also loved to cook, and he would make meals for everybody in the entire projects. He cooked for anybody at any time. He was such a giving guy, and strong as an ox. He was almost as strong as me, but not as big. He was muscular but skinny. He also loved to drink.

As a kid, I assumed Ricky's drinking was normal. I couldn't wait until I was older to be able to drink with him. It wasn't about the drinking or getting drunk; for me, I longed for the camaraderie with my brother. I didn't realize it was a problem until after I joined the military.

I was stationed in Fort Campbell at the same time Ricky was living in Nashville, only an hour away. One weekend when I was heading home to see Mama in Mississippi, I planned on picking up Ricky since he was on the way. At the time, I was an E5, and before I left on the trip, I ended up working duty that night. I was exhausted by the time I picked up Ricky.

"Bro—I'm really tired," I told him. "Like really, really tired. I've been up for twenty-four hours. Do you mind driving?"

With Ricky behind the wheel, I went to sleep right away. I was awakened by the sound of voices and the car engine shutting off. I knew we were stopped and could see the flashing lights of a patrol car behind us. As Ricky rolled down his window, a cop approached and looked down at him.

"Do you know how fast you were going?" the cop asked.

"No," my brother said.

"One hundred twenty miles an hour."

What the fuck, Ricky?

"Have you been drinking?" the cop asked him.

"Just a little bit."

As I would discover, "a little bit" for Ricky meant waking up and starting to drink. My brother was a functioning alcoholic. Even though my brother passed the sobriety test, he smelled like liquor, so they knew he shouldn't be driving. They booked him and told me I had two choices.

"You can just take your car and go on where you're going, or you can pick him up from the jailhouse in eight hours."

I couldn't leave him in the middle of nowhere. This was my brother. So I went to the jailhouse and waited all night for him. When they told me I had to pay his bond if I wanted to get him out, I explained I didn't have any money. Well, I had the money I was going to give my mother. I decided to use this to pay for his bail. Ricky didn't give me a big thank-you or anything. Of course, I never saw the money again, but I expected that.

Years after the drunk-driving episode, I came home to visit my brother in 2012, but by now I was acutely aware of his alcoholism. He drank all the time—from the time he woke up until the time he went to bed. He went to work drinking, he came home drinking. As the banquet manager at a popular hotel, it was too easy. He was an excellent cook. I called my brother a cook, but he really was a chef—he showed so much passion with it. He had shown me as a kid that black men could love to cook despite what my father thought.

When I saw Ricky in 2012, I talked to him for the first time as a grown man.

"Brother, I need you to stop drinking," I told him with tears in my eyes. "I don't want to lose you."

Ricky looked confused. "What are you talking about?"

He looked at me with conviction all over him that said he didn't have any problem.

"I don't want to lose you," I said again.

He saw how emotional I was, so he put his hand out and then grabbed me, hugging me and telling me things were fine. That he was okay. Several years passed, and after I came back home from Iraq, my sister told me with concern in her voice that I needed to come home and see Ricky. I told her I would, but I knew my brother was strong. He would be okay.

I had been having a hard time in Iraq, but it turned out Ricky was having an even harder time back home.

When I arrived at Ricky's place in Hampton, Virginia, I was surprised to see my entire family there. My mother and sisters and nieces and nephews—everybody. I was the last to drive up. They greeted me with hugs and smiles, so many whom I hadn't seen in a long time. The joy of the family reunion was cut short when I went inside to see my brother. Ricky was lying in his bed, and as I entered the room, the sight of him took my breath away. He weighed maybe ninety-five pounds at the most. The sickly figure in the bed could barely move. My heart dropped as I tried to muster a greeting, but I got a knot in my throat.

He's gone.

I left the room and told my family that I would be right back. Then I walked to the parking lot in front of the house and climbed into my car, knowing all their eyes were on me as I drove off just to control my nerves.

Fuck.

What did I just see? Who was that person in the bed? What happened to that beast of a brother? How had things gotten so bad?

How long have I been gone?

I wasn't gone long. When I came back to the house, I went in and talked to Ricky. I stayed for a couple of days. Right before I left, as I was in Ricky's bedroom saying goodbye to him, I asked if he was okay.

"Is there anything I can do for you?"

With a weak and soft voice, Ricky said, "You can give me some money."

"How much?"

"Three hundred dollars."

"I only have two hundred," I said.

He nodded and told me to give it to his wife, then asked if I could do a favor for him.

"Yeah, of course. What do you want?"

"Go in the kitchen and get me some whiskey."

My eyes watered up as I saw this shell of a man asking for the very thing that had killed him.

"Ricky—you know I can't get you no liquor. Why are you asking me for it? You don't need any more."

Even on his deathbed, unable to walk and barely able to move, he was asking for alcohol. As I left him and the rest of the family to head home, back to my life and job, I took the weight of this entire burden on my shoulders. I felt responsible yet couldn't do anything more. I couldn't will Ricky to live. I couldn't do a thing about his failing body. Two days after I left him, they admitted Ricky to hospice. Several days later, while he was in hospice, he made a decision that he told me about the last time my mother and I spoke to him on the phone.

"I don't want to die, Mama," he said.

Ricky passed away the next day.

After all those years of drinking the day away, of killing himself, he wanted to live and keep going. He held this desire inside of him for twenty-four hours, but it wasn't enough to save him.

★ ★ ★

My road to recovery had to be put on pause because of Ricky's death. Once again, I found a reason to fucking hate my soft heart. I could be dying but I'd pause death to help somebody else. I'd only continue dying once I knew I'd done what I could for that other person. It was like this so many times. I know that's why I'm the way I am now; I live for others.

People ask me, "What keeps you grounded, Chef?" I respond by saying, "You do." Others ask, "How do you keep going, Chef?" "'Cause of you. Thank you." Doing what I do now truly is therapeutic. When I look at the cliché that says it is better to give than to receive, I think that's a lie. I give *to* receive. I need to receive to keep giving.

When I first began my inpatient treatment, I began a journey of healing that Ricky never had the chance to start. He had run out of time, but time was all I had. I ended up being in two inpatients for six months, and then in an outpatient for a year. Nothing fucking worked, however.

The first thing they tried to do was medicate the hell out of me. I took a million pills, but none of them worked. I ingested everything—there wasn't a drug that you can think of that they didn't have me on at one point. I had always been a dominant person with a dominant personality, so the medication was in part an attempt to control me, to make me their puppet. They tried, but they couldn't control me. Instead, I attempted to control the situation as much as I could.

While I was in one inpatient in Texas, the same thing that happened to me in basic training when I first joined the Army happened once again. Even though I was there to help myself, I jumped into a leadership role to help others. There were men and women battling all sorts of things like PTSD, drug addiction, alcoholism, and much more. There are classes you take while you're there, and your time can be extended. So one month becomes another, then another. This happened to me, so the longer I was there the more of a leadership role I took, especially since I knew more than these guys and because I knew I was getting out. I started teaching classes myself, telling them what they should and shouldn't do. I started preaching basic leadership skills, and the staff hated that. Their attitude was *You can't do that,* but I was like, *Of course I can. I'm helping everybody!*

One day while I was at the inpatient facility in a class, someone asked me about one of the conversations I had shared with the group during a therapy session.

"Hey, Chef. What was the name of that general that you were talking about the other day?"

What an odd question, I thought as I told him the general's name.

"Do you know he's coming here tomorrow?" the guy told me, explaining that the former superintendent at West Point was doing a walk-through at the facility tomorrow.

"You're fucking lying," I said.

I decided to check with one of the nurses to see who was coming, and sure enough it was my former general. When she asked why, I told her it was nothing, but then it clicked with her. This was the man I had been talking about for some time, the same guy who had done things to help bring me there in the first place. Now this asshole was coming to a motherfucking inpatient with military members—males, females, Army, Navy, Air Force, Marines—saying that he wanted to help them. Right away the nurse understood the problem.

"Oh, no, no, no—we can't do that," she said. "He can't come here."

"No—let the general in. Let him come."

I wanted the general to come so I could see him up close and in person. The nurse knew this was a bad idea, and so did the rest of the staff. They stopped the general from coming without him ever knowing I was there. I couldn't believe the fucking irony of the situation.

The bad keeps winning.

There I was in inpatient care, putting my own personal growth on hold so I could help others who needed more help than me. Those suffering the most with PTSD or other issues. Yet this motherfucking general was coming in, acting like he really cared. All because of his title.

A rank can't reveal what's inside somebody's heart.

I was in Texas for four months, but it didn't do anything for me. All they seemed to be good at was pumping me full of drugs. I went to another inpatient facility in Virginia, and it was worse. The only difference was this second place medicated me even more.

There was this big and buff soldier at this place who they gave fifty milligrams of a drug, and he was out like a light, snoring. They gave me the same drug, same dose, and nothing happened. It was only when they gave me another fifty that it started to work. My body was fighting it. Slowly I calmed down, but the drug didn't knock me out. It just calmed me down enough for them to control me, to tell me to do whatever they wanted me to do. Every time I had a class, I came in like an extra on *The Walking Dead*. I was so fucking medicated. The guys would be telling me after the class, "Chef, wake up, man!" This went on for weeks.

Then my body decided to wake up. To wake *me* up. One day I had this split-second moment of resolution, where I came out of this stupor and thought, *Whoa . . . what the fuck is happening?*

I finally decided I wasn't going to take any more of this shit. Whatever this tiny moment of clarity was, it gave me enough to say, "No more." To tell the doctor that I was no longer supporting their billion-dollar industry that was draining us soldiers dry.

"You're full of shit," I told the young, black director while I was in his office for therapy. "You're not doing shit for these damn military men. All you're doing is taking their fucking money. I'm not fucking dumb. You're just taking their money."

He didn't particularly like that, but I didn't care. They were overmedicating me and everybody else. We'd be lined up in a row and then one by one walked up to a window where they gave us all the pills we had to take. You always had to open your mouth and show your tongue to prove you had taken them. I wasn't in treatment; I was in prison.

Once I came back home to DC and began outpatient treatment, the situation was no better. I was still in a prison, but it was one of my own making.

★   ★   ★

There has to be a point when you tell yourself there is a problem, and you make a pledge to stop. Not to press the pause button as I've done all my life but to pound a sledgehammer into the entire device and bash your will to bits.

After going through my inpatient treatment, I found myself medically retired from the Army and still going through outpatient therapy. I was still taking a handful of pills every day because that's what I thought I was supposed to do. I had also started to drink, to self-medicate, because that's what I thought I needed to do. But ultimately I had to be honest with myself. I needed a brutal and blunt conversation, not with Sergeant Rush and not with Chef Rush but with Andre Rush.

The stupid part about drinking was thinking that it would even help. I had never been a drinker; I gave it up after the incident in high school when my mother slapped me in the face. I didn't know what it was like to be drunk or have a hangover. They say that the more muscles you have when you drink alcohol, the quicker you become intoxicated, but that never happened to me. So I consumed a lot to accompany my big assortment of pills, a deadly and stupid combination.

Nothing worked. I know now that there is no magic pill you can take when you're in recovery. It's one thing to mend a broken body but another to rebuild a broken spirit. For me, I was still resisting letting go, still fighting a lot of internal demons. With my experience and my mindset, I had put up with so much bullshit, so it took a lot to tear down my stubborn walls and decide to make this fight my own. I needed something that was mine, so I reclaimed the spirit of determination.

One day there was another split-second realization, just like I had when I was an inpatient. I knew I needed to stop, to come clean and have the clarity of mind to fight this battle. I was taking around thirty pills every day, so I did the most dumb thing you could possibly do: I threw every single pill I had away. I grabbed the box the medication was in and dumped them all over the bed. Even if I had decided to wean myself off the drugs, the process would have taken months, since I was taking three times the amount a normal person would be taking. Months. I didn't have months. It was like my leg injury all over again.

I don't have six months to recover. I have to get better now.

I flushed all the drugs down the toilet. Of course, the withdrawal symptoms came quickly, and they were harsh and brutal.

I don't recommend my method of recovery, but I do advocate for my decision to make a change. Any change like this is drastic and requires a fierce determination. This was one of the times in my life I gave 100 percent to the task at hand. I wasn't competing in a game or a contest; I was fighting for my life.

★   ★   ★

All throughout this, I continued to cook. Early on in my life I didn't realize this, but even going back to my early days in the military and especially after 9/11, I had used cooking to cope. When I started catering, I went from three-course meals to four-course and seven-course and then suddenly it was twelve- and thirteen-course meals. People would be telling me, "Chef, you're fucking killing us. This is good as hell, but we don't eat like you." I didn't realize I was using this as a coping tool. Over the years, I began to show others how to use cooking to cope as well, even doing this when I was going through my inpatient treatment.

This was what I did. I showed the men and women dealing with PTSD how cooking could help them to cope. I would put a variety of food items in a mystery basket and give it to them, then I'd say, "Cook me some shit!" They would always look confused.

"Where's the recipe?" they'd ask.

"There's no recipe. It's right here."

Here we had all these alphas in the room, these strong males and females coming from all different backgrounds, some who knew how to cook and some who didn't. But they didn't want to cook like this. Their attitudes of confusion turned to *What the fuck, might as well try.* Then I noticed they would be asking each other what they were making and how they were doing it. Eventually the soldiers would be saying, "Look what I made" and then "Did you taste mine?" Soon the quiet kitchen was full of laughter. Some of them were gagging on their terrible dishes and while others thought theirs tasted pretty good. At the end every time, people loved it. The spouses and kids started taking part too.

Cooking to cope. Cooking to associate. There was an educational part to this, that you're not only learning how to cook but being strategic in what you're cooking. The food that you eat can be helpful with depression. Certain dishes help with high blood pressure and diabetes. I explained how to utilize food. I would take this a step further, to help teach people not only how to cook but also how to train their body. I would say, "You can't cook well if you can't have a great body like a chef!"

Of course, I wasn't Chef Rush. Not yet. Yes, I was a chef, but the official Chef Rush had not yet been born. All of my experiences had been my basic training before I could go and become the person I was born to be.

I still needed the opportunity to shine and the optimism to move forward. This came when I least expected it.

THE CHALLENGE COIN

Turn your wounds into wisdom.

OPRAH WINFREY

T his is what you're supposed to do.

I still hear my mother's words in my head, moving me forward.

Keep going. You can't stop now.

I still hold her wishes in my heart, motivating me in my footsteps.

My mother not only gave birth to Andre Rush, but she helped to conceive Chef Rush. If it wasn't for her encouragement, I wouldn't be here right now writing these words.

★ ★ ★

I should have never been at the White House on June 6, 2018. I wasn't even supposed to be working. In fact, nothing that happened that night was supposed to happen.

Then again, maybe it was all supposed to happen.

I had just gotten back from visiting my younger sister and nephew in Germany. Tomasina was a colonel in the Air Force. She's very intelligent, very diligent. She joined the military after I did and served in a couple different wars in Iraq and Afghanistan. I enjoyed making fun of her about being in the Air Force, since they say the Air Force is the most relaxed and caring of the military branches. Tomasina had been stationed at Ramstein Air Base in southwestern Germany for several years and had been asking me to come over to see her ever since she moved there. For almost three years I told her no, but after I retired from the Army, I no longer had an excuse.

"You know you're not doing anything," she said.

It was the truth. I was going through a lot of different things after leaving the Army, and Tomasina knew I had PTSD. She was aware that I was going through inpatient and outpatient counseling. So I finally decided to go see her.

My sister was proud of me. She knew what I had done and what I still could do. So when I was over there in Germany, she took care of me. She took me to Prague and we stayed in France for a while. It was good to be with family, to have distractions and to not be working so hard. When I left and got back to DC, I received a call from one of my White House colleagues right after getting home.

"Chef, come to work."

"I just got back from Germany," I said. The flight had been long, and I had jet lag. "I can't do it now. No way."

"POTUS is hosting a dinner for Ramadan," he explained. "It's kind of a big deal because he skipped it last year. POTUS is going to speak, and there'll be a ton of VIPs and press there. But it's going to be really simple. Really easy."

Even though I knew what the White House dinner consisted of, I still said no. Usually when the White House called, I jumped at the opportunity. I had been a chef there for over twenty years, serving four presidential administrations. I prided myself on being the guy they could count on for any event, no matter how easy or demanding it happened to be, but this time I said no.

My decision didn't last long. As I sat on the couch after the phone call, I realized I couldn't sleep, so I called back and told them I would come in.

I had been gone for a couple of weeks, so I couldn't find any chef's whites to wear to the gig. I owned close to two dozen sets of whites, but on this day all of them were missing or in the wash. The only chef jacket I could find had been given to me as a gift, and it was a jacket I never wore. The reason was because it had the name "Chef Rush" stitched in oversized letters on the right chest. I never wore whites with my name on them. You weren't supposed to have your name on your chef jacket, telling people who you were. In some cases, we didn't even wear whites at all. Not only did this jacket have my name on it, but "Chef Rush" had been printed an inch bigger than names usually were. I decided to go ahead and wear the jacket.

It's an easy dinner. No big deal. No one's gonna see me anyway.

The White House event was an iftar dinner. That's the ritual meal Muslims share to end their Ramadan fast. It's typically served after sunset. I had worked with a couple of other chefs all afternoon, putting the meal together, and so by the time early evening rolled around, most of our work was done. One of the guys said to me, "Hey, Chef, we're going to step outside to relax and pre-grill some of the veggies. Why don't you join us?"

"Nah," I said. "I'll finish up in here."

I never relaxed during a job, and I never went outside. The kitchen was my domain, and like a captain with his ship, I never deserted it until the gig was over. But that night, for no apparent reason, I thought, *Fuck it.* I stepped outside to enjoy the sunset and man the grill with my fellow cooks.

While we were in the lawn-and-patio area outside the West Wing, I immediately noticed a squadron of media people waiting outside the press room, so I moved to a different area to get out of their sight. I didn't want to deal with press. The two other chefs I was with talked to the media, but I didn't like the media. I'd been around it for a long time, so I was like a lot of people who knew how to jump in and jump out of a situation. I knew they were constantly digging for inside info, and I had a lot of inside info. But I do not share anything. Period.

I tried my best to make myself invisible, but this isn't an easy thing when you're my size. I could see these media people checking me out and whispering. Sure enough, they came wandering over, drawn by the smell of baby leeks caramelizing over charcoal. One of them asked me what we were cooking. I didn't mind answering his question; I'll answer questions about cooking all night long, just not about POTUS's eating habits. Then Kate Bennett of CNN asked if she could take a picture of the veggies.

"Knock yourself out," I said.

Right at that moment, a buzz went up among the media types. I guess POTUS was about to do his Q&A inside. All the media folks went stampeding in, and just before she joined the crowd, and unbeknownst to me, Kate Bennett snapped a photo of me standing by the grill. She had a little twinkle in her eye that made me nervous.

Fifteen minutes later, the press and some staff people started exiting again. Kate Bennett came marching up to me.

"I'm going to make you famous," she said.

"You do know that I'm already famous," I joked with her.

She smiled. "I'm serious. That picture I took of you is going viral."

"What picture?" I asked.

"The one I just posted on Twitter a few minutes ago," Kate said. "Look at your Twitter account if you don't believe me."

I gave her a smug look and said, "I don't have a Twitter account."

She looked astonished that I wasn't on social media. One of the other chefs said he was on Twitter, so he pulled out his phone and tapped on the screen for a few seconds.

"Chef!" he said, showing me his phone. "That's you!"

I stared at his phone screen, but I couldn't make sense of what my eyes were showing me: in the less than fifteen minutes since Kate Bennett had posted her tweet, there had been hundreds of thousands of "likes" and retweets. The number was climbing up in real time, like the digits on the National Debt Clock. My colleague was reading the comments on Twitter and both of them were laughing. I shook my head.

"Let's get back to fucking work," I said.

A few minutes later, we went back inside and the entire White House staff was buzzing about the tweet. The "White House Chef with the 24-inch Biceps" was becoming a meme right before my eyes. I'd never in a million years imagined I'd be the person in the middle of a viral internet event. Nor did I ever want to be. It was the most uncomfortable feeling because everybody was talking about me when I didn't want anyone to talk about me or even know me. I was always the one in the shadows, always the one hiding, and I was always the one pushing everybody else out in front. My job was to make everybody look good, and I was okay with being in the background always. Even when I was highlighted, I would always try to get out of the spotlight. This wasn't happening tonight. Everyone forgot about iftar; the only thing people wanted to talk about was that dumbass tweet about my biceps! Even POTUS was aware of it and making comments. The tweets hit the million-plus range before the evening was finished.

After I got home, I discovered I had made the evening news.

"Well, something positive came out of the White House and it wasn't Trump," the reporter said. "It came from the staff. And it was a chef, Chef Rush."

This will be over by the morning.

That's what I expected and hoped, but when I woke up, the viral avalanche hadn't slowed down. A fresh wave of tweets was going around, with photo captions like "America will win this arms race," "Nuclear arms," and "North Korea: We have nuclear weapons; White House: We have Chef Rush." Media like CNN began calling. Things were spinning out of control. And it all seemed so dumb to me. I felt there were bigger concerns the country needed to be focused on than some chef with big arms, yet I couldn't deny the whole thing was pretty exciting too. I thought it was a hoot, but I still didn't know what being a social media sensation meant.

I received a call from TMZ, so naturally I followed with "TMZ who?" They informed me they reported celebrity and entertainment news and wanted to do an interview with me. I said I couldn't go on and didn't explain why. They left me their number and told me to call if I changed my mind.

As this viral thing continued to spread like a forest fire, I realized I was back at the place I had been before going to Germany to see my sister. Seeing her and my nephew and visiting all those places took my mind off things, but they couldn't make me forget about things that cannot be forgotten. There I was sitting in the same spot on the couch I had been sitting on for the last two years. The same couch I wore a hole in not doing anything.

I knew I needed help, but God, did I hate asking for it. I decided to call my mother. I asked her how she was doing, knowing she wasn't on social media and had no idea about what was happening. So I started to tell her about everything that was going on. She said "okay" but I knew she didn't understand. It was nice talking to someone who didn't have an opinion, because everybody had an opinion. When I told her about TMZ and how they wanted me to do an interview, my mother said she had watched the show on television and thought it was humorous at times. Then she offered some advice.

"Pray over it," she said. "It may just be a blessing."

"Hmm. I'll think about it."

The next day as I was on my way back to the White House for another job, one of the staffers called me.

"Chef, maybe you should lay low till all this blows over."

Lay low?

This didn't sit too well with me. I'd done this long enough to know what this meant. Too much attention, even if it's not your fault, ends up being your fault. So let's make it an impactful mistake.

I realized there were two ways I could play this thing: the passive way or the active way. If I went the passive route, they'd control the process—the press, I mean. They'd ask their dumbass questions and make their dumbass little jokes, and I'd laugh and give my dumbass little answers. I'd have my fifteen minutes of fame until the next surfboard-riding granny or banjo-playing dog came along. Story over.

If I went the active route, though, I'd control the process. At least to some degree. I could use my fifteen minutes of fame to shine a spotlight on the issues and values that I think are important, and advocate my causes and concerns.

Option two sounded a lot better to me.

But to do that, I would have to get my head on straight. Fast. Before this train became a runaway. I would have to know what

I wanted to say when the cameras landed on me. And that would mean getting crystal clear about what was important to me.

As I steered my car onto Route 1 North, I started asking myself questions.

What does Chef Rush care about? What does he stand for? What are his values? Who the hell is this dude with the big-ass arms?

I decided to text TMZ back and agree to do an interview. When I did, one of them asked me if I had heard the news.

"What news?" I asked.

"Anthony Bourdain committed suicide," they told me.

I couldn't believe it. As I was trying to process the news, I discovered in the news where he had been when this happened. It was Kaysersberg, the same little town in Northeastern France that I had visited with my sister and left just a couple of days ago. I knew I needed to tell my mother this, so I called her again and told her the news.

"This is God's plan," Mom told me.

I call it divine intervention, I thought.

"Andre, this is what you're supposed to do."

My mother knew me, and she knew what I was going through. She was aware of the struggles I faced and the scars I carried. She knew what she meant when she said this was what I was supposed to do.

I needed to do the thing the superintendent never did for Sergeant Durden.

I need to speak up and say out loud the things people are going through. Things I've gone through.

I had never talked. We weren't allowed to talk. Social media was taboo. We didn't say anything. I decided that when I would talk, I would talk about positive things. I wanted to share about the good we can do and how we should be helping each other, about how we need to lift up one another.

Why can't I speak? I'm a fucking decorated combative. A retired master sergeant in the fucking military. I'm the actual shit. I don't give a fuck about accolades. I give a fuck about people, my country.

So I made a choice to speak. When I went on *TMZ Live*, I spoke the truth.

"I actually used cooking as a coping skill for me," I shared. "I myself had some things that were going on with me. I didn't know that cooking would be my tool until later on."

This was officially when Chef Rush was born. Now everybody would be calling me chef, dammit.

★ ★ ★

When I decided to become Chef Rush and join social media, I was entering a whole new world. I didn't have a Twitter account, so I decided to start one without having any idea what to do with it, how to run it, or how to do anything. I didn't know shit. I just knew it was an app and I could get on it. When I put Chef Rush as my name, guess what? It was already taken. There was another Chef Rush. And another. This was social media. Since I was trending, people wanted to take that away from me and use it to their advantage. I didn't realize this was how social media worked. Soon I discovered all sorts of vampires online: social vampires, energy vampires, moral vampires. So many people proved to be parasites. People stealing my name, starting websites with URLs that they offered to sell to me. *Keep the shit,* I thought. I would do it my way.

Not everything on social media was negative. Right after I got onto Twitter, I received a pretty cool direct message:

Chef Rush. I love what you're doing. Next time I'm in DC, we have to meet.

The message was from Arnold Schwarzenegger, the same guy who had played such a big part in my life growing up. He wasn't just a movie star to me. He had inspired me through his body-building and his book, *Encyclopedia of Modern Bodybuilding*. I replied and wrote, *Thank you. I appreciate that.* I had always been that way with celebrities that I met and served. I didn't take pictures with 99 percent of the people I had done things for because I wasn't there to do that. I served. I never wanted to seem like a groupie. So like I always did, I was polite and professional with Arnold, but didn't say anything more.

Not long after that, my cell phone rang and it was Arnold. His thick and unmistakable Austrian accent greeted me.

"Oh, Chef! Oh my gosh! You've got these huge pythons. And I thought that you were like a power lifter, but you do this thing with your body that is not like a power lifter." He poured out the praise over the phone. "You've got the whole package. The arms and the muscles and oh my God it's so amazing that you're doing this. We gotta get together."

I couldn't believe Arnold was calling me. I'm not one to be starstruck, but I was that day. Schwarzenegger reaching out to me was a game changer. Not only would I join Arnold to become an ambassador for his organization After-School All-Stars, which he created to help keep children safe and allow them to succeed in life, but he also encouraged me to set up my own program encouraging adults to integrate with kids as a means for personal growth and development. This eventually led to me starting my own nonprofit called 2222INC, where I bring military, first responders, and influencers together as role models providing direction and support for underprivileged kids (less fortunate kids from lower-income families).

The Army had trained me to work hard and to help. I had no idea that my life was about to become even more busy than it ever had been before. The busyness in the military—in the Pentagon and the White House and West Point and Iraq—didn't compare to how insane life was about to get for me.

★   ★   ★

A year after going viral and officially becoming Chef Rush, I was so fucking busy. I was on the road twenty-five days out of the month, traveling from East Coast to West Coast, talking to thousands and thousands of people. It was gratifying to know that I was helping and inspiring so many people, but it was also exhausting, especially after encountering the whole world of vampires and parasites that lurk online and on social media.

Everybody I was encountering were takers. Just takers. And the funny thing about it was that the takers thought that I was this big, dumb black jock, but one of the things that I became accustomed to and that I still do to this day is to play possum. A possum plays dead. So I can be in a situation and play stupid, playing into somebody's thinking about how I am and what their assumption might be. This shows me who they really are, their intentions, if they're true or they're not true. If they respect me as a person and my character, and what I stand for, or if they are thinking, *Let me take everything.* If they're wanting me to sign on the dotted line so they can own me their entire life. I've had so many of those come across my path, so many stories that they could fill an entire book. But let's not waste any ink on any of them.

One day I was with a kid doing a commercial with Gary Vaynerchuk, the successful entrepreneur, author, and internet personality. He needed seven people who were inspirational, and I was among those he picked to profile and showcase to his tens of millions of followers. What an honor. There were so many great people out there with inspiring messages, and he picked me. While I was there, I received a text from my sister:

You need to get home to see your mother if you ever want to see her alive again.

What the hell is she talking about?

I knew our mother was in the hospital, but there wasn't anything to worry about. I had been calling her and checking in to see how things were going. Of course, I was a mama's boy, and she didn't want me to worry about her. I hadn't been home to see her in a while because I was so busy doing my Chef Rush thing. Mama always reminded me that I was helping so many people, when we talked on the phone or when she left me messages.

"Baby, this is your mama calling you. I love you. Been following you on the Facebook. God bless you. Bye."

That was that last voicemail I ever received from my mother.

I rushed back to Jackson, Mississippi, and when I reached her room in the hospital, I realized how bad things had become. My sister and cousin were there. I sat beside her bed staring down at her. She couldn't talk and she looked feeble, having lost sixty or seventy pounds since I last saw her. She couldn't even move her head. A feeding tube was attached to her. As she looked up at me, her face grimaced in pain.

I was in shock. This was far worse than being surprised by Ricky's condition. I cried my ass off. My mother tried to hold my hand as her eyes looked up at me, wanting to console me, wanting to tell me things were all right. But she couldn't hide her hurt, and she was so sick she couldn't even shed a tear.

My sister and cousin told me they discovered my mother had bedsores that had been with her for weeks. Her entire body was raw. The nurses weren't even bothering to change her. I was so fucking disgusted at the care they gave to the elderly. We could see how in general people like my mother were pushed to the side as if they were nobody.

I left the hospital after a long day, weeping as I went back to my hotel to grab some food. This was the same hotel chain I'd been staying at for years, one I had spent thousands of dollars on because I traveled so much. After getting some dinner, I went to a table and sat back in a chair, only to feel it jerk back and flip me over. I fell on one side, landing hard on my wrist. I couldn't believe it. The pain was intense as my wrist swelled up.

The next day, my wrist felt even worse and looked even bigger. I went to the front desk and asked if they'd had any problems with those flimsy chairs in the dining room. They didn't seem a bit concerned, so I explained to them what happened, how I fell in one of their chairs last night and how my hand was now swollen.

"You guys need to check out those chairs," I told them. "What if that had been an elderly person? What if that had been a kid who was in that chair and it did that? What would have happened then?"

I wanted to talk to the manager, but I told them I had to go to the hospital instead to see my mother. I didn't have time for this shit. When I got to the hospital, I went to see my mother, who had not improved. As I sat by her bed crying over her, a nurse asked me what happened to my hand. After I told her, she asked if I wanted to get it checked out, so I did. They came back soon after with the results.

"Your hand is broken."

I couldn't believe it. They splinted it up. I spent as much time as I could with my mother that Saturday. While I was there, I received a call on my cell phone from the manager of the hotel, so I explained what happened and all she gave me was an "Okay, thanks" and then hung up. No apology, no concern, nothing.

That night when I returned to the hotel, the attitude was far different. Someone must have told them who I was, because all of a sudden, the manager and staff were asking me what they could do. "Mr. Rush, can we do anything for you?" They were going to pay for this and do that. It didn't matter. The damage had been done.

When I left the following day, I went to the hospital to see my mother. I kissed her goodbye, told her I loved her, and then said I would see her next week. On the plane back to Los Angeles, riding with the same splint on my hand, a white gentleman from Mississippi noticed it and when we got off the plane he asked me what had happened.

"You wouldn't believe it," I said with a grin.

"Try me."

After I told him the story, he handed me his card. "I'm a lawyer from Mississippi." I kept his information and eventually contacted him, giving him more information along with taking pictures of my hand, showing pictures of the damaged chair, and giving him any details I could. We went back and forth as he worked on the case, but the end result was that I couldn't do anything. He told me the popular hotel chain was fighting back, sending us pictures of a chair that wasn't even like the kind that had broken underneath me. They sent him a letter stating that his client swung his massive body into a chair that could only support 250 pounds, but they lied because I only weighed 230 at the time. They made excuses and everything, making it sound as if I had deliberately sat in a cheap chair and then had swung back in it on purpose. All while knowing that I was there to see my dying mother who was in the hospital.

I eventually let it go. I didn't care. I had stuff to do. I still have bills from that injury.

On the following Saturday as I was getting ready to travel back to see my mother, I received a text from one of my family members. It took me a moment to see that they were different hands, a rainbow of colors—black, dark, brown, and light—all touching my mother's hand. It was all my siblings surrounding my mother. I felt destroyed. I hadn't realized how little time she had left on this earth. I wish I had known. My sister told me that my mother didn't want me to know because she knew what I was doing for everyone and how much of an impact I was making.

My mother passed away on the anniversary of Chef Rush going viral. In honor of my mother's passing, I shared my thoughts on Instagram. I never talked about my family, but as I was in the airport holding back tears, I pulled out my phone and began to share about my mother. About how life is short, how we have to be more aware of our family, about how tomorrow is never promised. I shared my video with these accompanying words:

THE HARDEST THING I EVER POSTED.

-

Yesterday I had my year anniversary of becoming Chef Rush

-

Yesterday, I also had to say GOODBYE to my heart, lifeline that made me who I am, how I am . . . my mother

-

She was the person that pushed me, made me love hard, forget hate, racism, color, and always do what was right.

-

She knew she was leaving and she still pushed me on. She said "you have a purpose."

I saw my mother a few hours before her leaving this world. I
begged her not to leave me.

-

She was proud, she gave everything for me and I gave up my life
to help anyone.
#iloveyoumom #womenpower

★   ★   ★

My mother was buried on her birthday. To say I miss her is an
understatement. I remained strong that Saturday, but the following day, the doubts and inner demons began to seep in. I
found myself completely done, so done with every-fucking-
body. There were so many takers in this world and we had just
lost a giver in my mother. I couldn't deal with anything anymore. All I wanted to do was to go and sit on my couch in my
little hole. That's all I wanted to do. I knew I was talking to tens
of thousands of people and I knew I was reaching them, and I
also knew this voice inside of me telling me to quit was just me
being selfish. But at the moment I didn't care anymore. I wanted
to be left alone and go back to living a life of isolation.

Then something amazing happened.

Right as I sat there in self-doubt, grieving my mother and sulk-
ing in my distress, I started to get all these messages from everywhere. Thousands of them. Notifications and comments and
posts and everything on all my social media. I was even getting
texts and calls. I had no fucking idea what was going on until I
looked and saw that I had gone viral again. Not in a small way,
but a huge way. I found people talking about me on Reddit and
in foreign countries. It was everywhere. I couldn't believe it.

I can't even mourn my fucking mother. She just passed away and now I have to deal with this.

The irony was that this wasn't because of something new I had posted or that someone else had shared. This was coming from an old picture that had been out there for a year.

At first I was mad. No, not just mad, but furious. My mother was gone and I wasn't even being allowed to have some moments to myself to process this. The anger inside of me burned for a moment, but then I felt this coolness rush over me, extinguishing the flames and calming my soul. It was then that I realized what had happened. I looked up at the sky and smiled.

"You did this," I said to my mother. "You did this."

That picture of me had been one of her favorites, and it had been out there forever. And it just so happened that twenty-four hours after she passed away, this photo went viral. Everybody was once again talking about Chef Rush. I knew this was my mother talking to me.

"Keep going, Andre. You can't stop now."

Every good part of Emma D. Rush lives inside of me, and the best parts are the ones meant to be shared with others. Even on her deathbed with her last remaining breaths, she told me to keep going. She wanted me to inspire not just one person but everyone. She wanted me to make a difference and to never forget to give back.

I've done this, Mother. I'm doing it. And I'm going to keep doing it.

Shortly after this, I made a coin to remind myself and share with others what my mother was reminding me of when this post went viral. On the front of the coin were three things my mother used to always say to me.

"You can do anything. Never give up. Keep going."

She was always selfless in her work, whether she was in the kitchen or simply cheering us on in the background. She always urged me to keep on doing God's work, as she liked to call it.

On the back of the coin are the important parts of me, the pieces that solve the puzzle when put together.

"Inspiring The World." That phrase hangs above a globe of the earth to remind everybody that we are one. To treat everyone the same. To remember that no one is better than the next person.

"Mental Health. 2,222 Push-Ups A Day."

This goes along with the flexed arm. Have you seen my arms? I've used them to advocate for suicide awareness and prevention in the military and among civilians, combating a stigma created by decades of misconceptions. This flexed arm also ties into one of my passions: physical fitness. This is as crucial in today's world as mental health. Most importantly, the flexed arm is for the women in the world, because like my mother, they are the strongest of us all.

"Celebrity Chef."

This goes with the image of the chef's hat, which is a way of saying that it doesn't matter if you wear a suit and a tie or if you're a garbage man. You can make a difference. The image of the kids in a circle on the back of the coin also ties into being a celebrity chef. My desire is to encourage "no bullying." Kids have to go through a lot, not just bullying but cyberbullying and the effects of social media on their mental health. There is no age limit in addressing this.

"Combat Vet."

In the middle of back side of the coin is my bronze star, which is a reminder to never forget that everyone has a story, and every person's life can make a difference. It doesn't matter who you are and what you do.

This coin was made in the shape of a weight plate. There's one more phrase on the back of the coin:

"Because Of You I Didn't Give Up."

This coin was made in memory of my mother and the mission she gave me.

This is what you're supposed to do, Dre.

Okay, Mama. I still hear you. I love you. Thank you—I know this now.

Keep going. You can't stop now.

EPILOGUE

★ ★ ★

There are certain questions I'm almost always asked. Like the following: "So what do the presidents like to eat?"

I've been asked this ever since starting to work for the White House, which seems like a lifetime ago, and it's a common query when serving presidents, DVQs (distinguished visitors' quarters), queens, kings, and senior military leaders since starting in 1997. This isn't the important question, because I will feed the president the same way I feed a homeless person. Actually, I take that back. I'll feed the homeless person better, because the president gets the best service all the time. The menu a president picks out is fun to discuss, but the more important thing is what goes on behind that menu. It's the thing that has driven me throughout my entire career and the reason I got to the White House in the first place.

It's about passion and service. An interest in the culinary arts brought me into this arena, but a desire to give 100 percent to everybody I served propelled me to where I'm at now. Being a chef is all about service. It goes back to what my mother showed me in the kitchen. It wasn't just the warm, delicious meals she made, food that I always try to mimic but still don't ever perfect like she did. People will tell me some dish of mine is incredible, but I'll tell them it's not like what my mom made. She did, however, impart to me the knowledge that cooking wasn't just about the meal, but the meaning behind it. My mother's cooking gave you a feeling of belonging, a feeling of togetherness, and that is what I always strive to give to others. I don't want you to just taste my food—I want you to *feel* my food. I don't care how good it tastes, because I know it's going to taste good. I want you to feel it, to take away that same feeling I used to have when I ate my mother's cooking.

When you approach anything with a servant heart, you will be successful. For me, the service isn't only in the culinary world. When I'm doing an ice carving, I'm making kids smile. If I'm speaking to a crowd, I can see the interest and response in the audience. Everything I do is a service, even with the social media I post. The key with this is to never become complacent. Don't ever become too comfortable and think that your service is extraordinary. You have to work hard every single day.

So maybe you work your butt off but you still never find success. How have I been able to find success? For me, I have listened to and learned from people I admire and have worked with. Going back to a hero of mine whose book inspired me as a kid, Arnold Schwarzenegger has provided a road map for me in so many ways, and he's even given a list of how to become successful. In 2009, Schwarzenegger shared six rules of success at the commencement address for the University of Southern California. That's a starting point for anybody, so I'll share them with you.

Arnold Schwarzenegger's Six Rules for Success

1. Trust yourself.
2. Break some rules.
3. Don't be afraid to fail.
4. Ignore the naysayers.

5. Work like hell.
6. Give something back.

I've followed these rules my whole life and added a few.

I've trusted myself, sometimes too many times. Sometimes I've followed my dumb ass down stubborn roads, but I've remained true to myself. You are your greatest ally.

Yeah, I've broken some rules. I've broken protocol. I've helped those in need and stood up for those who needed an advocate. Sometimes in life you have to make your own rules.

Failure has never been a fear of mine. What I've learned over the years about failing is that it will make you stronger, so you must trust the process, even when you're down and being counted out.

Ignore the naysayers. That could be the title of this book, dammit! That's all I've done my entire life, from proving to my father that I could lift that car to standing up to that grade school bully. The Army naysayers, the military naysayers, the critics in the kitchen and the skeptics in the gym, from the Pentagon to West Point, and now from Instagram to Facebook . . . Yeah. It's only you against yourself, so follow your heart.

Work like hell? Hell, yes! I've worked like hell for the Army, for presidents, for generals. Now I'm working like hell for others, for you, to give something back. Doing 2,222 push-ups a day doesn't just happen. It takes day after day after day of hard fucking work.

For the sixth and final rule, I feel like I've been giving back my whole life. That's what chefs do. We don't become chefs to become celebrities; a chef and a cook are those who love to serve others, who love to give back and create something for people, like my mother did.

Those are keys to success. I will add another, a big one for me. Every day I press the reset button and begin again. I treat it like it's my first day. My first time on the job, my first time speaking in front of a crowd, the first time I'm meeting someone. I've spent my whole life pressing the pause button, but I press the reset button even more.

There are lots of haters out there waiting to cut you down. Just the other day, I received a message from an online hater that said to me, "Just remember, you'll always be nobody, bro." I responded with "You're right, but I'll be that nobody that everyone remembers." Another online vampire who was hating on me wrote, "Now go in the back and get me some coffee, Chef." I wrote to him, "This is how simple and ignorant you are. I'm not the Chef who gets the coffee. I'm the chef that owns the whole building."

Every now and then I have to show someone that I'm a bad motherfucker. Sometimes I sit back and reflect on my life with a sense of awe.

What the fuck, Dre? You've done all these different things with all these different people all over the world. From cooking to exercise to carving ice sculptures to being a pastry chef and a chocolatier and a sommelier. You're into bodybuilding and fitness and the military and the kids and all these different things you stand for, and you still get fucking shit for no reason.

But that's just the nature of the beast.

You have to always remember your worth, but at the same time, you have to always stay humble.

I think back to the young baker full of energy and limited on knowledge. So raw but so restless to learn. A humble kid with big dreams. I keep him in my mind. No—I'm not talking about my younger self. I'm talking about Sergeant Durden. I took him under my wing and was hard on him, hard enough to break a man, but later he thanked me and shared his story. From then on his story became my story. So I worked him even harder, gave him goals and drive, and told him what he was going to do even when he had doubts.

I taught Sergeant Durden a lot, but he taught me more. His life revealed to me that reality is hard sometimes, but we must always reflect and remember the hardships, even during the best of times. It's how we survive, thrive, and continue in those dark periods that define us.

I say this all the time: I wear this chef jacket to make sure I stay humble. I do it not only for the kids and not only for the military but for anybody I'm talking to and encountering. Staying humble is always remembering where you came from and what you didn't have. I'm from Columbus, Mississippi, a place where I would walk for miles to work in raggedy old shoes. I lost my southern accent but never my heart. Always remember where you came from, but at the same time, never forget your true worth.

My parents never let me forget where I came from, and they always let me know my true worth.

When I left to go to the Army, my dad told me to make sure I kept in touch with the family, and I did. But he taught me a valuable lesson one time I came back home to visit. I had already been in the military for several years. On the first day I came back home, I didn't see my dad because I was with friends, and the same thing happened on the second day. On the third day of being home, I finally saw my dad. He wasn't exactly pleased to see me.

"What's wrong with you?" he said to me after I greeted him.

"Sir?"

"What's wrong with you?" he repeated. "You go off and you act like you're somebody different. You come back home and you're out with your friends, you're out doing this and that, and you don't even have time to see your mother and me."

As my dad went off on me, I was at a loss. Why was he so angry? He was such a forceful and intimidating guy, and even though I was an adult now with my own place and my own job and my own life, he still intimidated me. He was still the head of the family, and he should be respected. I had thought that, since I was only coming home for a few days, I could spend time having fun with my friends. I had seen my mom and given her some money, but that wasn't enough.

"Dre—seeing your mother isn't about the money," my dad told me. "Time is something you never, ever get back. Family is something you never can replace. When your mother's gone, when I'm gone, you'll never get back those moments you could have had. Remember that."

My dad was right; I would never get them back. I did come back home because of my mom—spending three or four days with her, taking her to dinner, bringing her gifts—but I didn't spend as much time with her as I should have. But Mom never complained. She told me to go out and see my friends. "You have a good time."

After my dad's blistering rant about spending time with him and my mom, I went to my room. Twenty minutes later, my mom came knocking on my door.

"Yes, ma'am," I said.

"Can I come in?" Mom asked.

"I'm really kind of busy."

She walked in anyway and smiled. "So am I."

Mom saw the look on my face, so she sat down beside me and grabbed my hands, rubbing them with her thumbs and palms. Her hands were always so soft; I think that's why I keep my hands soft, because I never want to forget the way my mom would rub my hands whenever she wanted to talk to me. It was a form of endearment, and it was soothing to feel her smooth hands going back and forth over mine.

"You know, Andre, your dad only wants what's best for you. You know why he's the way he is. You know how your dad grew up. You know how your dad did everything. You know, we didn't have much when I was your age. We didn't have the things that you have now."

I couldn't help but think, *You didn't have the things I have now? Then you really must not have had anything!*

"Wow, that's really nothing, Mom."

"Yeah, that was nothing, but we had each other," she said. "We had each other. Your dad just wants you to be the man that you deserve to be and that you need to be. Many of the kids have had their chances but you—you're different. You had a chance to see everything that they did right and all the things they did wrong. Now's it's up to you. You can listen, or you don't have to listen. But it's up to you to make that difference. I've learned that if you fail, you're going to fail. You'll succeed if you're going to succeed. I know you'll do both, but I also know that you'll do the right thing. Your dad just wants to see you do the right things. I know sometimes he doesn't express it the way that you want to hear it, because it was never expressed that way to him. But he never had a chance because he stopped being a kid in fifth grade and was forced to be a man."

My mom was showing me that every day I was given a chance and an opportunity to make the right choices and to succeed and to try to make a difference with my life. So that's the same advice I'm leaving with you.

It's a brand new day today. It's your chance to do something extraordinary.

But first, drop right now and give me 2,222, dammit!

ACKNOWLEDGMENTS

★ ★ ★

This book came from a source deep down inside of me, a storehouse of memories kidnapped, held hostage, and tortured. It took the mindset, hearts, and strength of many to pull these stories out of the dark.

To my father, Tommy Lee Miller. Thank you for making me the strongest man I never knew I could be, physically, emotionally, mentally.

To my sisters and brothers on both sides of the family. Thanks to every one of you individually, as you each gave me a lesson of worth, love, and understanding. We are all we have; let's stay together.

To my kids. I live and breathe for you guys. You make me so proud. I am your biggest fan, and you are my role models. Thank you.

To my nephew, Deadrian Buckhalter, gone too soon. I'm grateful for the eternal smile you left the family in your memory.

To Renee. Thank you from the bottom of my heart. I could not have done this without your support, and I can never repay you.

To my extended family, thank you for always cheering me on.

To Wesley Durden. You gave everything and received little. Thank you for letting me be your voice. RIP.

To Arnold Schwarzenegger. Thank you for showing and giving me a platform of greater giving. For putting me in front to shine brighter than the sun. And for displaying the know-how to combat any naysayers.

To Dan Solomon, Jake Woods, Rob Wilkins, and the Mr. Olympia family. Thank you for making me part of greatness and adopting me into a sport that you knew I belonged in and would represent with pride.

To Eric the Trainer (Eric Fleishman) and Alysha Kanemoto. There are not enough thank-yous I can give to express how grateful I am to you both. You've made me so much greater, and you are my family.

To TJ Millard and my ETT gym buddies. Thank you guys for being positive 24/7. Many days, I've depended on you when you didn't even know it.

To Mike, Mona, Kali, AJ, Scott, Pasha, Chris, Rob, and all my other fitness friends and influencers who have shared everything with me. Thank you.

To Mark. Thanks for giving me a home to train in ETT.

To Chef Rich Mutz. Thank you, Chef. You grew me in the culinary arts. My first Olympics was everything.

To Tony and my CAT family, you guys kick butt! Literally.

To Travis Thrasher. Thank you for making me realize my story in words.

To the teams at Harper Horizon and The Fedd Agency, especially Amanda, Andrea, Esther, and Danielle. Thank you for bringing this book to life.

To my friends, fans, supporters, military, and all . . . Thank you for all the love and believing in me like I do you.

To all the kids, no matter your color, no matter your environment, lack of opportunities . . . I'm thanking you now for not giving up and keeping going.

And to Columbus, Mississippi. Thank you. I wouldn't have changed a thing.

ABOUT THE AUTHOR

* * *

CHEF ANDRE RUSH was born in the small town of Columbus, Mississippi. His father was a country farmer. Young Andre developed his love of fresh food by working on the farm and his love of cooking by helping his mom create family dinners. He was a gifted artist, football player, and record-breaking track star whose skills earned him an Olympic tryout. But cooking was always his true passion.

As a young man, he joined the US Army Reserves, where his physical strength and leadership abilities were singled out on day one. This led Rush to join active duty and into a whirlwind of growth. He also served as a minuteman, a combative trainer, and a military fitness endurance trainer. However, it was via cooking that he made his strongest mark.

During his military years, Rush won hundreds of medals for cooking, culinary Olympics, ice sculpting, and other related skills. His reputation as a cook led to a call from the Pentagon to try out for a job in the Joint Chiefs of Staff kitchen. He got the position, which led to his first cooking opportunity at the White House. While working at the Pentagon and White House, Rush also developed a private business on the side, catering parties for Washington society.

Chef was at the Pentagon the day the plane struck the building on September 11, 2001. He was part of the recovery effort and as a result later suffered PTSD symptoms, which instilled in him a passion for helping America's wounded warriors.

Today, Chef has his hands in many pies, literally and figuratively. He has been a key advocate for the USO, Fisher House, Veterans of Foreign Wars, and American Legion, as well as an active supporter of the President's Council on Fitness, Sports, and Nutrition. He is currently developing his consumer-driven brand, which will include his food line, health/wellness/fitness products, apparel, his 501(c)(3) 2222INC, and more. He recently contracted with Gordon Ramsay's Studio Ramsay production company to host a new series, which he has begun working on.